Happy About® Global Software Test Automation

A Discussion of Software Testing for Executives

By Hung Q. Nguyen
Michael Hackett
Brent K. Whitlock

21265 Stevens Creek Blvd.
Suite 205
Cupertino, CA 95014

Happy About® Global Software Test Automation: A Discussion of Software Testing for Executives

First Printing, August 2006
Tradebook ISBN 1-60005-011-5
Place of Publication: Silicon Valley, California, USA
Library of Congress Control Number: 2006927989

Trademarks

Warning and Disclaimer

Publisher and Executive Editor

- Mitchell Levy, http://www.happyabout.info/

Copy Editor

- Jennifer Finger, President, Keen Reader http://www.keenreader.com/

Cover Designer

- Malcolm Turk, http://www.flickerinc.com/

Layout Designer

- Val Swisher, President, Oak Hill Corporation
  http://www.oakhillcorporation.com/

A Message From Happy About®

Thank you for your purchase of this Happy About book. It is available online at http://happyabout.info/globalswtestautomation.php or at other online and physical bookstores.

- Please contact us for quantity discounts at sales@happyabout.info
- If you want to be informed by e-mail of upcoming Happy About® books, please e-mail bookupdate@happyabout.info
- If you want to contribute to upcoming Happy About® books, please go to http://happyabout.info/contribute/
- Please see our web page http://www.happyabout.info/globalswtestautomation.php and our Wiki http://www.happyabout.info/wiki/SoftwareTesting

Happy About is interested in you if you are an author that would like to submit a non-fiction book proposal or a corporation that would like to have a book written for you. Please contact us by e-mail editorial@happyabout.info or phone (1-408-257-3000).

Other Happy About books available include:

- Happy About Joint Venturing: http://happyabout.info/jointventuring.php
- Happy About LinkedIn for Recruiting: http://happyabout.info/linkedin4recruiting.php
- Happy About Website Payments with PayPal http://happyabout.info/paypal.php
- Happy About Outsourcing http://happyabout.info/outsourcing.php
- Happy About Knowing What to Expect in 2006 http://happyabout.info/economy.php

Other soon-to-be-released Happy About books include:

- Happy About CEO Excellence: http://happyabout.info/ceo-excellence.php
- Happy About Working After 60: http://happyabout.info/working-after-60.php
- Happy About Open Source: http://happyabout.info/opensource.php

Acknowledgments

Thanks to Hans Buwalda for vision and leadership on test automation in general, and Action Based Testing specifically, as well as his contribution in the automation discussion of this book.

Thanks to Jesse Watkins-Gibbs for all the help.

Thanks to Mitchell Levy for support and patience in enabling us writing this great book.

Thanks to LogiGear for supporting us on this project.

Thanks to Scott Allan for his comprehensive review of the book.

Thanks to all those who contributed their insights and experience to the pages of this book.

Thanks to everyone else who helped us along the way.

Dedication

This book is dedicated to all executives, managers and engineers who have the will, courage and determination to deliver excellent products through employing sound business sense, thoughtful strategy, better coding and intelligent testing practices.

contents

1

The Business Side of Software Testing

Why you should read this book

As an executive, it is your job to set the strategic direction for your company to succeed in the marketplace. You need to set strategies for marketing, sales, R&D, finance, IT, human resources, and support services. In a software company, test strategies are as essential to business success as software development strategies. Despite their importance, most companies lack explicit software test strategies and frequently suffer from poor product quality and release schedule adherence. This book was written to highlight the critical issues associated with software testing and quality assurance that impact the effectiveness of your company's executive staff and bottom line, and to share a strategy that can improve them. An effective test strategy can do this by improving the visibility into the quality of your company's products, so that you can make better management decisions, lower your testing costs, and accelerate your time to market.

No matter your role, we suggest that you read chapter 1.

- If you are a **CEO, COO, or on the executive team,** you should also read chapter 6. Browsing the other chapters gives you more information on testing issues, but is not necessary.
- If you are a **CFO**, you should read chapters 3, 4, and 5. Browsing chapter 6 is suggested.

If you are the VP of Engineering or responsible for testing in your company, we highly recommend that you spend time on chapter 6. You might also find chapters 2-5 useful.

Introduction

This book addresses five core questions surrounding testing:

1. Why should you care about and spend money on testing?
2. Why must you treat testing as a strategic effort?
3. Why should testing have its own properly funded budget, separate from development?
4. Why must you have better visibility into quality and testing effectiveness?
5. Why is Global Test Automation your best-practice solution?

These questions address the elements of quality (customer satisfaction) and money (spending the least amount of money to prevent future loss). The bottom line in business is money (making more and/or spending less). Ultimately, the benefits of effective software testing boil down to increasing your revenue or decreasing your costs, both of which directly impact the bottom line.

1. Why should you care about and spend money on testing?

Testing takes time and effort which will cost varying amounts of money, based on the magnitude of each. The objective of testing is to improve the quality of your software, which leads to better customer satisfaction, which indirectly leads to higher revenue. This is a classic case where spending money is necessary to make money. The goal of this book is not to advocate that you spend so much money on software testing that you break the bank. We agree with the general goals that most companies have of minimizing both the time and cost devoted to testing, and will show you how it can be done while achieving your quality goals.

When the software testing effort can give you confidence in the quality of your software, you can sleep better at night.

2. Why must you treat testing as a strategic effort?

Testing is an integral part of the product development process for software applications. Ensuring that your product meets its quality objectives is necessary, so that it will meet your customers' expectations and be commercially successful. Testing is actually a large part of the overall product release budget. Our internal studies have shown that software development accounts for up to 40% of the typical product release budget, and software testing accounts for up to 40% of the software development budget for companies that develop software for sale.

With consistent quality products that meet customer needs in a user-friendly manner, you end up with the following benefits:

1. Happy customers
2. Happy sales staff
3. Living up to your marketing claims

4. Timely delivery to sales channels and customers
5. Elimination of embarrassments

Treating software testing as a strategic effort will allow you to turn quality into a competitive advantage.

3. **Why should testing have its own properly funded budget, separate from development?**

In many companies today, software testing is still typically tacked onto the end of the software development project. This is absolutely not appropriate! With the services that testing performs that differentiate it from software development, and the relatively large amount of financial resources that are devoted to it in relation to software development, it really should be treated as a project of its own. This will allow the software testing team to effectively interface with the software development team instead of being subservient to them. To do that, a separate budget is necessary. This helps prevent it from getting shortchanged when the product development effort goes over budget or is running behind schedule.

When testing gets shortchanged to make up for cost and schedule problems in software development, then product quality is shortchanged. This increasingly repeated cycle will force you to release a low to marginal quality product that will ultimately end up hurting your sales and reputation. Releasing a software product with bugs has hidden costs associated with fixing them after it is in the customers' hands. Unfortunately, your development staff ends up rushing to fix the bugs and trying to keep your customers happy instead of developing new features for the next release.

Figure 1 shows how a typical software development and testing team plan for software testing as part of a product development lifecycle. There are two fundamental problems associated with testing: first, testing happens too late in the process; and second, the schedule is built on the hope that software will be delivered to testing on time with no changes.

The Testing Problem—What We Plan

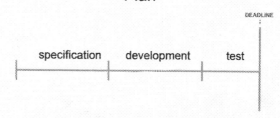

Figure 1:   The testing schedule as part of a typical product development lifecycle.

The reality is reflected in Figure 2, as is well-known in the software industry. While it would certainly be desirable for the development staff to deliver code on time with no changes, reality makes that highly unlikely. This book has been written to provide the guidance needed to strategically structure effective testing and test automation programs that adapt to the reality of software development.

The Testing Problem—What Actually Happens

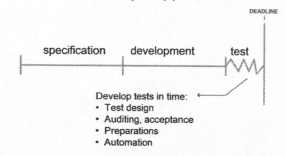

Figure 2:   What actually happens to testing in the typical product development lifecycle.

4. **Why must you have better visibility into quality and testing effectiveness?**

Testing performs several functions for the benefit of the company, the product development effort, and the executive team. Testing is a service to the company to help it produce and release higher quality software. Testing is also a service to the development team to help it produce higher quality code. For the executive team, testing should be an information service that provides visibility into the software product quality for effective management. We always say that when the software testing effort can give you confidence in the quality of your software, you can sleep better at night.

Some of the key internal values achieved through effective testing and QA are:

1. Confidence in consistency and dependability
2. Ability to spend more time on new development, less time on maintenance
3. Effective utilization of resources and budget
4. There's time and money left over that can either flow to the bottom line or be used to increase productivity
5. Elimination of surprises

5. Why is Global Test Automation your best-practice solution?

All elements of business rely on two fundamental resources: time and money. The goal of this book is to share a solution that will allow you to optimize your resources while increasing quality. The 2 by 2 matrix in Figure 3 shows the tradeoff between the approaches detailed in this book along the axis of time and money.

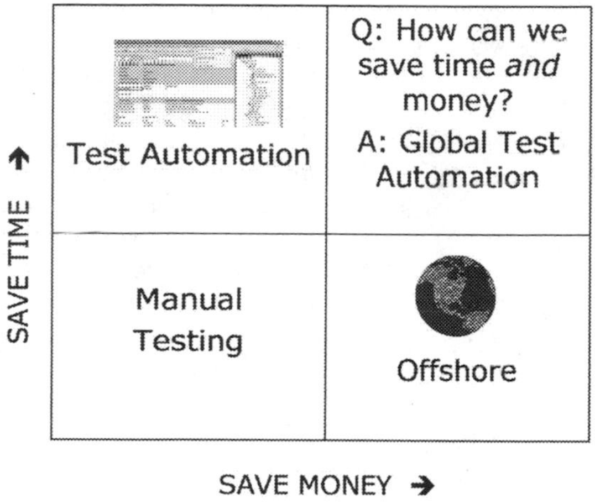

Figure 3: The Global Test Automation 2 by 2 Matrix.

You can save time by automating testing. You can save money by offshoring. Both approaches have associated issues that are detailed in chapters 4 and 5 respectively. If you want to increase quality while saving both time and money, Global Test Automation is the solution. Global Test Automation provides strategic integration of technology, speeds up the testing process, and provides a distributed team to achieve your objectives.

The strategic integration of technology and a distributed team speeds up the test process, saves money, and provides the needed results. With the power of the Global Test Automation strategy, 1+1=3.

Global Test Automation is the *integration* of the latest test automation methodologies and technologies with global resource strategies to fully capitalize on the speed, cost advantages, and best practices in automation and global sourcing. Its *structured approach* is based on a methodology known as Action-Based Testing (ABT), which creates a hierarchical test development model. ABT allows test engineers (domain experts who may not be skilled in coding) to focus on developing executable tests based on action keywords, while automation engineers (highly skilled technically but who may not be good at developing effective tests) focus on developing the low-level scripts that implement the keyword-based actions used by the test experts. This seamlessly allows the best utilization of the skill sets of your staff back home as well as offshore staff. The ABT methodology has been proven for over a decade in Europe, and has now gained traction and popularity in the US. We will explain further in chapter 6.

Summary

Software testing should have its own budget and be properly funded because it is:

- A service to the company to help it produce and release higher quality software products.
- A service to the development team to help it produce higher quality code.
- An information service to the executive to provide visibility into the software product quality and enable more effective management.
- An enabler to help you sleep better at night.

Driving toward the solution

In the rest of this book, we discuss the following:

- An overview of software testing
- The pitfalls of manual software testing and some suggestions for improvement
- The pitfalls of software test automation and some suggestions for improvement
- The pitfalls of outsourcing/offshoring and some suggestions for improvement
- The Global Test Automation strategy
- Case studies and quotes from experience in these areas

2 An Overview of Software Testing

In this chapter, we will present an overview of software testing, including the following points:

- Its relationship with Quality Assurance
- The benefits of the visibility that software testing provides executives
- Metrics used in software testing
- The concept of Quality Cost
- Types of software testing
- The products of software testing
- The activities in software testing
- Common misconceptions about software testing
- The relationship between software development methodologies and software testing
- Suggestions that can help with software testing
- Case studies in software testing

Introduction

Software testing is an integral part of the software product development process. At the same time, it is not a subset of software development. Unfortunately, many people think of it as a footnote, and don't give it the attention or respect that it requires. Software testing is more than that—it is in fact a discipline in its own right. In this chapter, we present an overview of software testing to provide a framework of understanding for the subsequent material in the rest of this book.

Relationship with Quality Assurance

"I feel that QA is perhaps the most important part of software development and sadly the most neglected – either due to a time or resource crunch."
*— **Shyamsundar Eranky**, Symbol Technology*

Testing is not quality assurance. It is an essential part, but quality assurance encompasses and requires so much more. By definition, quality assurance is the assurance of the quality of a product. No matter how much you test a product, you cannot test quality into it. Testing can assess the level of quality of the software by identifying defects. Other steps must be taken to reduce the defects (e.g., bugs) and assure that the software is of the desired quality.

To assure high quality software, one must begin at the beginning with a quality development process. From project initiation and requirements definition through software design and development, all steps share ownership of quality and must have quality as an objective. Assuring quality includes assembling a talented development staff and providing continuous training to keep their skills current while they develop new skills. These things are as important as good testing to the release of a high quality product. The key here is holding the development team accountable for the code quality. In the development process, the engineering team does unit testing of the code before it ever gets into the hands of the QA staff. When the QA staff does its testing, they can measure the first-pass quality by categorizing and counting the bugs, and this can be used as a metric for the development team's code quality.

Quality assurance requires a budget for resources and authority to set standards and solve problems. The *real* head of QA can send programmers to courses in effective software engineering. The role includes prevention as well as late-stage damage control. In many companies, the *real* head of QA is the President or a Senior Vice-President.[1]

If you as an executive rely on the word of your software development team that the software is high quality and ready for delivery, you may be rudely awakened to reality when your customers claim otherwise.

Visibility

Testing provides a major benefit to the executive: visibility into the status, that is, the maturity and readiness for release or production, and quality of the software product under development. The visibility that is provided enables management of the software development process, with measurements of the quality and completeness of the product. In a sense, software testing is an information service. For example, regression testing provides information about changes in the software from build to build. Testing finds and reports bugs, identifies weak areas in the software, and identifies high-risk areas of the project. Testing reports explain findings in ways that help engineering solve problems, the customer service staff assist customers, and management make

---

1. C. Kaner, J. Falk, and H. Q. Nguyen, *Testing Computer Software, 2nd Edition.* (New York: John Wiley & Sons, Inc, 1999), 347.

sound business decisions regarding each bug. Testing provides the executives with the information needed to manage the product development. The more information available to executives, the better the software will be. Ultimately, this speeds up the product development process and lowers the overall cost, so it is worth the cost to do it right.

If you as an executive rely on the word of your software development team that the software is high-quality and ready for delivery, you may be rudely awakened to reality when your customers claim otherwise. This is not to say that your software development team is not trustworthy, but a fresh set of eyes, skilled in software testing with a different perspective, is essential. If your customers find the bugs and problems instead of your own software test team before it is released, you have the headache of getting the problem fixed in a hurry while you try to appease the customer and control the damage. This can damage your reputation and relationships with your customers, and ultimately cost you business. The visibility provided by good software testing also provides peace of mind, as it drastically reduces the likelihood of problems like these.

From the tail end of development through release, it is the test group that gives you the clearest visibility into your product. Your goal is to get the best view of the product your investment can buy. You want to make sure that the software testing organization is well-funded and competent to give you adequate information in a timely manner. Timeliness is important here, as you want visibility in the present, not the past. To improve testing, think of how you can get more information faster, and more cost-effectively. This is a challenge—while a software development project can be managed to be essentially finite, testing is infinite due to the infinite combinations of software input, paths, and hardware/software platform combinations. It is this great unknown in software testing that can make executives lose sleep at night. We will discuss this in the coming chapters.

After the release of the product, any bugs that impact customers must be found quickly and addressed quickly. The speed with which you get information on bugs and failures in a released product is important, because you then need to perform an analysis to identify the root cause of the bug or failure in the code, and a root cause analysis to determine why the bug slipped through testing and ended up in the released product. These activities take time and effort, while the customer simultaneously pressures you to fix the bug. A bug or failure that appears in the released product takes at least twice as much work to fix, and costs in terms of time and financial pressure to fix it are much greater than if it's been found prior to release.

Metrics

Metrics are the means by which the software quality can be measured; they give you confidence in the product. You may consider these product management indicators, which can be either quantitative or qualitative. They are typically the providers of the visibility you need.

Metrics usually fall into a few categories: project management (which includes process efficiency) and process improvement. People are often confused about what metrics they should be using. You may use different metrics for different purposes. For example, you may have a set of metrics that you use to evaluate the output of your test team. One such metric may be the project management measure of the number of bugs found. Others may be an efficiency measure of the number of test cases written, or the number of tests executed in a given period of time.

The goal is to choose metrics that will help you understand the state of your product.

Ultimately, when you consider the value of a metric, you need to ask if it provides visibility into the software product's quality. Metrics are only useful if they help you to make sound business decisions in a timely manner. If the relevancy or integrity of a metric cannot be justified, don't use it. Consider, for example, how management analysis and control makes use of financial reports such as P/L, cash flow, ratios, job costing, etc. These reports help you navigate your business in a timely manner. Engineering metrics are analogous, providing data to help perform analyses and control the development process. However, your engineers may not be the right people to give you the metrics you need to help in making business decisions, because they are not trained financial analysts. As an executive, you need to determine what metrics you want and tell your staff to provide them.

For example, coverage metrics are essential for your team. Coverage is the measure of some amount of testing. You could have requirements coverage metrics, platform coverage metrics, path coverage metrics, scenario coverage metrics, or even test plan coverage metrics, to name a few. Cem Kaner lists over 100 types of coverage measures in his paper "Software Negligence and Testing Coverage."[2] Before the project starts, it is important to come to agreement on how you will measure test coverage. Obviously, the more coverage of a certain type, the less risk associated with that type.

The goal is to choose metrics that will help you understand the *state* of your product. Wisely choose a handful of these metrics specific to your type of project and use them to give you visibility into how close the product is to release. The test group needs to be providing you plenty of useful information with these metrics.

The goal of understanding quality costs is to analyze where you spend your money/time/budget to get the most bang for the buck.

---

2. C. Kaner, "Software Negligence and Testing Coverage," *Proceedings of STAR96 (Fifth International Conference on Software Testing, Analysis, and Review)*, Orlando, FL, May 16, 1996, p. 313.

Quality Cost

While testing is only one aspect of quality assurance, it represents by far the largest cost associated with quality, *quality cost*, in most organizations. Quality cost is the sum of all costs a company invests into the release of a *quality* product. There are four types of quality costs: prevention costs, appraisal costs, internal failure costs, and external failure costs.

1. **Prevention costs represent everything a company spends to prevent software errors, documentation errors, and other product-related errors.** These include requirements and usability analysis, for example. Dollars spent on prevention costs are the most effective quality dollars, because preventing errors from getting into the product is much cheaper than fixing errors later. If there is an error in a requirement or the intended usability, and money is spent on developing the software to the erroneous requirement, the costs of identifying the error, determining how to fix it, and then developing new code to correct it will arise later.

2. **Appraisal costs include the money spent on the actual testing activity.** Any and all activities associated with searching for errors in the software and associated product materials falls into this category. This includes all testing: by the developers themselves, by an internal test team, and by an outsourced software test organization. This also includes all associated hardware, software, labor, and other costs. Once a product is in the coding phases, the goal is to get the most effective appraisal job, so that internal failure work is streamlined and well-managed and prevents skyrocketing external failure costs.

3. **Internal failure costs are the costs of coping with errors discovered during development and testing.** These are bugs found before the product is released. As we mentioned previously, the further in the development process the errors are discovered, the more

costly they are to fix. So the later the errors are discovered, the higher their associated internal failure costs will be.

4. **External failure costs are the costs of coping with errors discovered after the product is released.** These are typically errors found by your customers. These costs can be much higher than internal failure costs, because the stakes are much higher. These costs include post-release customer and technical support. Errors at this stage can also be costly in terms of your company's reputation and may lead to lost customers.

The table in Figure 4 shows examples of costs that fall into each of the four categories of quality costs.

Prevention	Appraisal
Staff training	Design review
Requirements analysis	Code inspection
Early prototyping	Glass box testing
Fault tolerant design	Black box testing
Defensive programming	Beta testing
Usability analysis	Test automation
Accurate internal	Usability testing
documentation	Pre-release out-of-box
Pre-purchase evaluation of	testing by customer service
the reliability	staff
of development tools	
Internal Failure	**External Failure**
Bug fixes	Technical support calls
Regression testing	Answer books (for support)
Wasted in-house user time	Investigating complaints
Wasted tester time	Refunds and recalls
Wasted writer time	Interim bug fix releases
Wasted marketer time	Shipping product updates
Wasted advertisements	Warranty, liability costs
Direct cost of late shipment	PR to soften bad reviews
Opportunity cost of late	Lost sales
shipment	Lost customer goodwill
	Supporting multiple
	versions in the field
	Reseller discounts to keep
	them selling the product

Figure 4:   The four categories of quality costs.

All the costs mentioned above can be effectively reduced through smarter test efforts that include a high degree of test automation.[3] Test automation when done *right* leads to greater test coverage, resulting in higher-quality products. Higher-quality products require less technical support, fewer patches, and lead to greater customer satisfaction. Smarter automated testing also speeds up the release process and incrementally reduces the manual test costs. But most of all, more test coverage gives you and your customers more confidence in your product. You'll be able to sleep better at night not having to worry about whether there are bugs lurking in your software that haven't been exposed yet because of insufficient test coverage, and whether you'll have to scramble at the last minute (typically on the first day of that much-needed vacation you've been planning all year), to deal with the problem and fix it to your customer's satisfaction in a rush.

The solution to quality cost problems is to get a better understanding of your investment in product quality and manage your costs better. The first place most organizations look for a better understanding is in the highest cost area: the software test effort or lack thereof. For example, if you don't test at all, your testing or appraisal cost is low. You will ship on time but your external failure costs will skyrocket. Your prevention and appraisal costs will result in finding errors that can be corrected while they are still internal failures, where they are cheaper to deal with than when they are external failures.

The goal of understanding quality costs is to analyze where you spend your time and money to *get the most bang for the buck*. It is well known that it is faster and cheaper to find and fix a bug during unit testing done by developers early in the development cycle. Should we then spend most of our time/budget on unit testing? No. There are many limitations to unit testing. Unit testing is not capable of finding many varieties of bugs, including graphical user interface (GUI) bugs,

---

3. J. M. Juran, *Quality Control Handbook, 3rd Edition*. New York: McGraw Hill, 1974.

usability problems, end-to-end bugs, and configuration bugs. For most organizations, getting a better unit test effort will help you release a better product sooner. It is not a replacement for the test effort done by skilled software testers, but it may reduce the time that test effort takes. Understanding quality costs will hopefully help you shift some of your test effort to the most cost-effective places.

In the graph in Figure 5, the total quality cost is shown in the upper bathtub-shaped curve. On the bottom axis is the quality of performance, ranging from totally defective to zero defects. On the left axis is the cost per good unit of product. You can see that with highly defective software, your prevention and appraisal costs are very low, but your failure costs are very high, yielding a high total quality cost. With zero defect software, likewise, your failure costs are very low, but your prevention and appraisal costs are very high. To optimize your total quality costs, you want to be between these extremes, at the bottom of the bathtub curve.

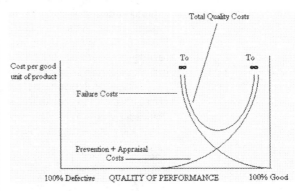

Figure 5: Theoretical model of optimum quality cost.

This offers two challenges: First, a sufficiently sophisticated accounting system allowing a typical mid-sized company to track the total cost of quality has yet to be developed. To optimize total quality cost, you need to have the appropriate categories in your accounting system and keep track of the related costs.

Chapter 2: An Overview of Software Testing

Second, you need to be able to track your external quality costs. You may not even have enough information from customers on why the software isn't working for them. How are you going to know what to book into your accounting system for external failure costs? The point here is that while capturing this data is difficult and expensive, you know that the benefit is reducing your overall cost of quality. You need to determine if the benefits of tracking your total quality cost will give you enough of a return on investment to make setting up the appropriate accounting system and paying for the implementation of the program worthwhile.

An Example of Quality Cost

Consider an example of the theoretical model of optimum quality cost, shown in Figure 6. In this example, there are three scenarios presented. In Scenario 1, a fair amount of money is spent in prevention and appraisal. This amount is actually higher than both Scenario 2 and Scenario 3. The result is that Scenario 1 has the lowest external failure costs of the three scenarios. Scenario 1 does have higher internal failure costs than the other scenarios, but that is understandable because testing results in finding bugs, and they cost money to fix. In Scenario 2, no money is spent on prevention, and only a little on appraisal. Yet, that scenario has the highest total quality cost because the total failure costs far outweigh any savings in prevention and appraisal costs. In Scenario 3, more money is spent on prevention than in the other two scenarios, and a mid-range amount is spent on appraisal compared to the other scenarios. Likewise, a mid-range internal failure cost results for Scenario 3, and a mid-range external failure cost results for Scenario 3 as well. But, Scenario 3 results in the lowest total quality cost. Scenario 3 is the best scenario because it balances these four types of quality costs the best for the lowest total quality cost.

	$ Scenario 1	%	$ Scenario 2	%	$ Scenario 3	%
Prevention	$ 10,000.00	3%	$ -	0%	$ 20,000.00	6%
Training	$ 10,000.00	3%	$ -	0%	$ 20,000.00	6%
Appraisal	$ 130,000.00	36%	$ 30,000.00	5%	$ 90,000.00	26%
Testing	$ 130,000.00	36%	$ 30,000.00	5%	$ 90,000.00	26%
Total Prevention + Appraisal	$ 140,000.00	38%	$ 30,000.00	5%	$ 110,000.00	32%
Internal Failure	$ 150,000.00	41%	$ 40,000.00	7%	$ 142,000.00	42%
Bug fixing	$ 120,000.00	33%	$ 30,000.00	5%	$ 115,000.00	34%
Regression test on fixes	$ 30,000.00	8%	$ 10,000.00	2%	$ 27,000.00	8%
External Failure	$ 75,000.00	21%	$ 495,000.00	88%	$ 90,000.00	26%
Technical Support	$ 60,000.00	16%	$ 450,000.00	80%	$ 70,000.00	20%
Returns	$ 15,000.00	4%	$ 45,000.00	8%	$ 20,000.00	6%
Total Failure	$ 225,000.00	62%	$ 535,000.00	95%	$ 232,000.00	68%
TOTAL QUALITY COST	$ 365,000.00	100%	$ 565,000.00	100%	$ 342,000.00	100%

Figure 6: Quality Cost example.

Types of Software Testing

So far, we have mentioned manual software testing and automated software testing. These names describe the mechanism by which the testing is performed, not the intrinsic nature of the tests themselves. There are a number of types of software testing, categorized by what is being tested and the purpose, or objective, of the test. The objectives range from usability to disaster recovery. For many organizations the most common testing types are: functionality testing, compatibility testing, performance testing, scalability testing, usability testing, application security testing, accessibility testing, and regulatory-compliance testing. A short list is given below.

1. QA Testing—Loosely defined vernacular for a combination of requirements-based, regression and feature level testing performed during post code-delivered phases such as the system, integration and final test phase, to assess and assure the quality of the product.

NOTE Currently, the term "QA testing" is widely used, or misused rather, to refer to functionality validation and verification testing. This is technically incorrect, but since its use is pervasive, we'd like to offer a definition for it.

2. Functionality, or feature-level, testing is performed to verify the proper functionality of the software. It may include testing of the mathematical and algorithm correctness of scientific and financial software, as well as testing of GUI functionality.

3. Compatibility testing ensures that the software is compatible with the hardware, operating systems, and other software packages that it will be working with.

4. Performance testing determines how well the software performs in terms of the speed of computations or responsiveness to the user.

5. Scalability testing is performed to ensure that the software will function well as the number of users, size of data sets, or other factors change from small to large values.

6. Usability testing ensures that the software has a good level of ease of use.

7. Application security testing determines how well the software can defend against attacks, such as firewall software securing a computer against Internet viruses and worms.

8. Accessibility testing is performed to ensure that the software will be accessible under various scenarios by the intended users.

9. Regulatory-compliance testing is performed to ensure that the software is in compliance with all applicable regulations.

While the objectives and methods for conducting each of these types of tests are different, we will focus on QA testing in this book.

The Products of Software Testing

Just as software development is a process that results in products, namely software products, software testing is a process that results in products. These include the following:

1. The test design process produces a series of test cases.
2. The test execution process produces a list of software anomalies.
3. The problem identification process produces bug reports.

Corresponding with the three products of the software testing process, three main activities define software testing. These include the following:

1. Designing the software tests.
2. Running these tests.
3. Identifying problems that come to light through the test execution.

All three of these activities carry a heavy responsibility of communication with the product development team, as well as company executives, to establish confidence in the product. Effective and meaningful communication back to these teams can often be problematic for test teams that do not have or follow defined company processes or standards, are continually pressed to cut the test time, or are working with development groups that do not have a full appreciation of the testing, do not understand its purpose, or feel that testing is a roadblock to release.

By thinking of testing as producing products, and considering these products as assets, an organization's approach to testing can be significantly enhanced.

Usually, organizations think of testing as an activity as opposed to a product. It is seen in terms of costs and savings, as the activity costs money but finding bugs early saves money. By thinking of testing as producing products, and considering these products as assets, an organization's approach to testing can be significantly enhanced. Consider the following points that come out of this way of thinking:

- Test cases have a definite value and can depreciate over time as the underlying application changes.
- Well-written test cases consolidate the intellectual property of your team members and retain that knowledge in the company as staff members may come and go.
- Well-automated tests can be re-used over and over again, becoming assets that produce profits for the company.

What Makes Good Testing?

Good testing starts with providing proper methodology, environment and the funding to carry it through. Designing good tests requires training and good project management. The test team should be involved in the requirements review process to gain a solid understanding of the product, and begin designing tests early in the development process. For test teams that rely on manual software testing, execution of the tests consumes most of their time on a project; this time commitment is often the most significant problem the development organization faces.

If the product requirements are not well-defined, or the schedule slips or becomes too tight, the development organization may cut or eliminate the time allocated for designing tests and exploratory testing may be performed immediately instead. This causes project management problems and a loss of confidence in the product of the testing process. The rest of the development organization then has no assurance of what the test team is doing, and the test team can only rely on their gut instincts for what tests they perform, since they have not gone through the necessary process of designing good tests. While gut instinct does have a role in software testing, it does not engender confidence in the product of software testing when it is used as its basis. You should run as many effective and well-designed tests that address high risk and important areas as you need, to give you the most meaningful visibility and confidence and enable you to sleep well at night.

"A great majority of software tests are designed to confirm the existence of features, instead of attempting to break the software."
— **Sue Kunz**, *CEO of Solidware Technologies*

What makes up good test designs? Validation, the confirmation that the software indeed provides the features that were specified, is not sufficient for testing. Software testing is more than validation. Indeed, it is important to do more than validate the software, and in some cases, even more important to attempt to break the software than validate it.

The objective of testing a program is to find problems. The purpose of finding problems is to get them fixed. The point of the exercise is quality improvement.

For example, if you are releasing a limited-functionality demo version of your software for free distribution on the web, it is vastly more important to attempt to break the software to ensure that you cannot access the features reserved for the full version of the software than it is to confirm the existence of the features that are supposed to be there. Imagine the financial loss if you accidentally left the key functionality of your expensive software in the give-away version.

Most testers spin their wheels doing validation, but that doesn't really improve the *quality* of the software. Quality control/validation is only a subset of *testing*. It is a different discipline. Testing sees if the software works in the manner that the customer wants it to, and does not break even when the user makes mistakes or misuses the product. Validation checks that the software meets the requirements.

The time investment in test execution is the largest single quality cost for most development organizations today, and is well understood. Cutting this time is the highest priority for most organizations, but has typically met with poor results. For example, this has resulted in a lack of confidence in the product. While it is not expected that testing will find every bug, which it can't do, many companies have nothing more than their good wishes and hopes that the software they release is of substantive quality, won't damage their reputation, or result in a customer support nightmare. In addition, cutting the test execution time often results in poor communication due to the resulting changes in approved test plans and coverage matrices that make development teams wonder what is going on in testing. Since most of this occurs at the end of the development cycle, there is a feeling that testing is an albatross on development.

The test team should have a number of things to enable management to make better decisions regarding product quality. These include the following:

- Effective training.
- Continuous skills development.
- Efficient implementation of test tools.
- More effective communication from the test team to the product development team and management.

Higher quality products from the test team relieves management stress and fosters better decision-making.

Common Misconceptions About Software Testing

Some common misconceptions about software testing are related to how software testing differs from other testing. Here we discuss five types of common misconceptions:

1. **You can completely test the system.** This is impossible because there are too many combinations of data and user input and program paths, as well as hardware or software platforms on which the tested product runs, to allow complete testing in a reasonable period of time.

2. **You can have "zero defect" or bug-free software.** There is simply not enough time and money to test everything. The goal is to test well enough to deliver "good enough" software quality. In addition, no matter how good your software may be, it runs on an operating system with bugs, with device drivers that have bugs, on computer hardware that has bugs, etc. The bugs in the environment on which your software runs can cause problems in your software. And since there is a virtually infinite variety of computer hardware and operating systems (and their associated bugs) on which your software may be run by your customers, there is no way to test them all.

3. **Software testing is exclusively a quality control activity.** Actually, software testing is partly a quality assurance (QA) and quality control (QC) activity. Quality control refers to measurement or inspection activities that are intended to compare the actual results with the expected results of a project. This is only a subset of software testing, as QC rarely takes the

customer's needs as a priority. Possible examples of QC-related testing include regression testing. In actuality, software testing is a process of exploration in which there is an iterative evolving process of test design, execution, and problem identification.

4. **Software testing slows us down.** Product release schedules have been driven very hard by forces such as the need to be first to market, putting extreme pressure on the speed of development. When project schedules slip, testing gets squeezed the most. There have been great advances in software development platforms and tools, both proprietary and available as shareware, open source, or freeware, that significantly accelerate the development process. In addition, software development methodologies such as Agile and Extreme Programming speed up software development. However, traditional testing has not kept pace with these advances, and has not experienced a corresponding increase in speed. This leads to the perception that testing slows us down, as it hasn't sped up as the development process has.

5. **Software testing is software development.** While it is part of the overall software development process, it is actually a very separate function. It is common to use software development, software design, and programming interchangeably. It is not, however, common to say "software development" when you mean "software testing." Consider this illustration: often, people think of sales and marketing together. The two words are often spoken together, as if to describe a single function: the generation of revenue. However, these are two very different activities. Marketing spends money, which could be viewed as an indirect sales activity because it ultimately generates leads and opportunities that turn into revenue. Sales, however, makes money because it brings in booked revenue. Likewise, software development is a creative activity which

results in the generation of an eventual product, which in turn will generate revenue. It is directly constructive. Testing, however, is a destructive activity in which problems in the product under development are brought to light. Testing costs money, yet the results can lead to delays in the product release and eventual revenue.

Budgeting for Testing

Like sales and marketing, software development and software testing need to have two separate budgets as they are two separate functions. There needs to be some independence between the software test group and the software development group. By having separate budgets, budget overruns in development are not as likely to result in equal budget cuts in test, which would result in the detriment of the overall software product quality and success. By having separate budgets, testing also feels less like an albatross. Not having its own line item on the budget can lead to that feeling, because it feels like testing is taking resources that aren't allocated for it. Testing can account for 10% to 50% of the overall software product development budget.

Relationship Between Software Development Methodologies and Testing

It may surprise you that a standard like CMM does not solve the testing problem. Adherence to Carnegie-Mellon University's Software Engineering Institute's Capability Maturity Models may help development organizations release higher quality software. However, this methodology focuses on doing things right, but not necessary the right thing. The overhead is very high. It might be appropriate for a very large development house with big budget, but might not fit with a development team of less than a hundred. The certification process is very expensive and laborious. It includes various levels of certification that do not guarantee better software products. It also doesn't focus on software test planning or execution. This surprises some in the software development arena. CMM-certified organizations can become so process-heavy that product release schedules significantly slow down. In fact, some organizations that may be certified at the CMM level 5 may choose to operate at a lower level, such as CMM level 3, for particular projects in order to reduce the burdensome processes and speed up their development schedule. There is no guarantee that a focus on the quality of the process will result in a higher quality software product.

Executives need to recognize the separation between testing and development, just as they do between sales and marketing. While methodologies and standards such as CMM, Agile, Extreme Programming (XP), Scrum, etc. can help with software development, there are different things that can help with testing. The following things can help with testing:

1. Get a better understanding of the test process.

2. Increase your test coverage.

3. Optimize your investment in manual testing.

4. Maximize the effectiveness of test automation.

These can have a huge and immediate impact, even if incremental. These can give you more confidence in the software product and how it will be received by the market.

Bugs are tested out, but quality must be built in.

Steven Yang, *CEO of MathScore*, contributed the following:

"I view the presence of a large QA staff to be a symptom of a poorly developed product. After all, if a product were both well-designed and well-written, there simply wouldn't be a lot of testing required. In most companies, it is true that an alarmingly high percentage of development resources goes into software maintenance, such as bug identification and bug fixes. Some developers believe this cost can be as high as 90%. Once you run into this problem, is the solution to improve the quality of your testing, or is the solution to rewrite the buggy code? Although rewriting code is time consuming, I have never regretted a single decision to rewrite code. In fact, a code rewrite often results in a superior architecture due to a better understanding of the product. You have to fix the source of a problem, and unfortunately, a code rewrite is usually the superior fix. Otherwise, repeated testing and bug patches may lead to disastrously unmaintainable code.

"In my opinion, if the code base is both well-written and well-designed, at least 90% of developer time can be consistently devoted to new development, even after a product is multiple years old. That is the case with MathScore.com. When code is truly solid, the time spent to build an automated test harness might not even achieve a suitable return on time invested. Furthermore, if you have to fix a major bug, you should rewrite the code, which means you'll have to rewrite the test harness. Even worse than that, automated test harnesses never anticipate obscure bugs, which are usually the ones that are tough to fix. Although automated test harnesses can be useful, I've found manual testing to be more cost-effective.

"The natural follow-up question, of course, is why isn't more code well-written and well- designed? Writing code well is a skill that can be acquired through training. It does not require genius intelligence. However, I estimate that less than 10% of all senior developers write good enough code to be useful teachers, and nearly 0% of them are given an opportunity at a company to train others. This is the single most important skill that can be taught, and there are numerous books about software engineering that teach this skill. It is unfortunate that so few companies understand that training in the art of software construction can have a dramatic impact on the quality of a development team and software product. Design skills are a different beast, however. Reading books and learning from others certainly help, but the best designers are simply more talented than everybody else. Quite literally, if you want a great product, get a very smart person to design it.

"To summarize, the best form of testing is prevention through superior development techniques."

Summary

In this chapter, we discussed the following:

1. Software testing is a discipline in its own right.

2. Testing is an information service to the executive that provides visibility into the status of a product through the choice of appropriate metrics.

3. Testing needs its own budget with sufficient funds allocated to it.

4. Testing represents the largest quality cost in most organizations.

5. Quality costs should be minimized by optimizing the balance of prevention, appraisal, internal failure, and external failure costs.

6. The products of software testing are valuable assets to your organization.

7. Bugs are tested out, but quality must be built in.

It is worth the investment to do testing right, aside from building in quality throughout the development life cycle. Increased quality leads to increased incremental revenue and savings in the costs of low quality. Increased speed of getting a quality product to market also results in increased incremental revenue. A higher-quality product increases sales through better customer acceptance, as well as reviews and word-of-mouth advertising. A higher-quality product also cuts technical support and customer support costs while also relieving management headaches. A proper budget and funding for testing and QA is necessary. It should be a line item in the P/L section of the budget.

By doing testing right, it feels less like an albatross on product development and more like a service to delivering better software. Effective automated testing can be a better test solution than manual testing, and cut the largest quality cost. Better solutions for testing will also incrementally increase the speed with which new products are released.

Driving toward the solution

In the following three chapters, we will discuss the following pitfalls of software testing:

- The Pitfalls of Manual Software Testing
- The Pitfalls of Software Test Automation
- The Pitfalls of Outsourcing/Offshoring Software Testing

In Chapter 6, we will present the Global Test Automation strategy, an approach that avoids these pitfalls and enables you to capitalize on the value that software testing can provide.

3 The Pitfalls of Manual Software Testing

In this chapter, we will present the top five pitfalls of manual software testing, listed below:

1. Manual testing is slow and costly.
2. Manual tests don't scale well.
3. Manual testing is not consistent or repeatable.
4. Lack of training
5. Testing is difficult to manage

We will then present the top five suggestions, listed below:

1. Be thorough in test design and documentation.
2. Automate the turnkey tests as much as possible.
3. Manage the test activities well.
4. Rank test cases in order of importance.
5. Have a separate budget with proper funding for testing.

We will then present some case studies that illustrate the issues.

Introduction

Manual software testing has been the cornerstone of software testing. All test engineers and software QA staff, software engineers, developers, and programmers test their code manually, at least to some degree. Manual software testing is employed with all sizes of projects and budgets, ranging from zero to billions of dollars. It is a critical element of software testing, but not the be-all and end-all. Furthermore, it is not synonymous with quality assurance. Just as in software development, the quality of the results of manual software testing can vary widely depending on many factors.

The Top Five Pitfalls of Manual Software Testing

Manual software testing is a necessity, and an unavoidable part of the software product development process. How much testing you do manually, as compared to using test automation, can make the difference between a project's success and failure. We will discuss test automation in more detail in a later chapter, but the top five pitfalls of manual software testing illuminate areas where improvements can be made. The pitfalls are listed and described below.

1. **Manual testing is slow and costly**. Because it is very labor-intensive, it takes a long time to complete tests. To try to accelerate testing, you may increase the headcount of the test organization. This increases the labor as well as the communication costs.

2. **Manual tests don't scale well**. As the complexity of the software increases, the complexity of the testing problem grows exponentially. If tests are detailed and must be performed manually, performing them can take quite a bit of time and effort. This leads to an increase in the total time devoted to testing as well as the total cost of testing. Even with these

increases in the time and cost, the test coverage goes down as the complexity goes up because of the exponential growth rate.

3. **Manual testing is not consistent or repeatable**. Variations in how the tests are performed are inevitable, for various reasons. One tester may approach and perform a certain test differently from another, resulting in different results on the same test, because the tests are not being performed identically. As another example, if there are differences in the location a mouse is pointed when its button is clicked, or how fast operations are performed, these could potentially produce different results.

4. **Lack of training is a common problem, although not unique to manual software testing**. The staff should be well-trained in the different phases of software testing:
   - Test design
   - Test execution
   - Test result evaluation

5. **Testing is difficult to manage**. There are more unknowns and greater uncertainty in testing than in code development. Modern software development practices are well-structured, but if you don't have sufficient structure in testing, it will be difficult to manage. Consider a case in which the development phase of a project schedule slips. Since manual software testing takes more time, more resources, and is costly, that schedule slip can be difficult to manage. A delay in getting the software to the test team on schedule can result in significant wasted resources. Manual testing, as well as badly designed automated testing, are also not agile. Therefore, changes in test focus or product requirements make these efforts even more difficult to manage.

The Top Five Suggestions

There are ways that pitfalls associated with manual software testing can be avoided or resolved. In this section, we discuss five of these.

1. **Be thorough in test design and documentation**. In designing the tests, there should be agreement among the business staff, product and project managers, developers, and testers on test coverage. This can be documented as test requirements in a test plan. With this documentation, management can have visibility into the test coverage and know that the right areas are being tested. This then becomes an important management tool in managing testing.

The goal is to find the easiest way to document as many test cases as possible without having the test effort turn into a documentation effort.

Have the test requirements and test cases peer-reviewed, just as you would have software design reviews. The software development staff and the test staff should jointly develop the test designs, as they have complementary skill sets and knowledge bases.

In manual testing, like in other processes, several factors influence the effectiveness of the tests, including the completeness of the test cases and the thoroughness of the documentation. The goal should be to maximize management's understanding of the testing by spending the appropriate resources in each area, within the overall resource constraints. If you don't document your tests, you won't understand the coverage or software quality as revealed by the tests, and you also won't be able to determine that the test team is testing features that are the most important to your development team and customers. However, if you document everything related to each test case, you won't have time to do as many tests as you should. Documenting test cases can get expensive. The goal is to find the easiest way to document as many test cases as possible, without having the test effort turn into a documentation effort.

2. **Automate the turnkey tests as much as possible**. There are various tools available that support test automation. When it is cost-effective and time-efficient to do so, there is no excuse for not automating software tests. The benefit of automation is that the testing becomes less burdensome, and less likely to be scrimped on when under pressure. This also makes the testing easier to manage.

"Software testing is surprisingly low-tech, and requires too much 'hands-on.' Would most people run their virus software frequently if they had to invoke it manually?"
—***Sue Kunz***, *CEO of SolidWare Technologies*

---

3. **Manage the test activities well**. Do this as closely, and by establishing as full a procedure, as the software development activities. Be sure that the project plan has sufficient resources and time allocated to testing so that it doesn't get short shrift.

4. **Rank test cases in order of importance, by impact on quality, by risk, by how often the feature tested is used, or some other related metric**. A goal should be to run all important test cases, but if there are resource constraints that prevent all test cases from being run, then the ranking will enable the important test cases to be run. This provides the maximum impact of the testing with the available resources. In manual software testing, you are always short on time. There should be an agreement or signoff procedure on the ranking and the coverage of the tests.

5. **Have a separate budget with proper funding allocated for testing**. Just as there is a budget allocated for the software code development, there should be a budget allocated for testing. Be sure that this budget is well-funded. Watch how much is spent on testing, and what the return on investment is.

Even when you have a good test automation program in place, you will still need to do some manual testing. The usability testing, for example, requires human involvement. However, manual testing is not the solution for short-cycle, high-volume test challenges. For example, if you have a daily build process where you need to run smoke-tests to assess the changes and stability of the software from build to build, these tests can be high-volume and short-cycle. Manual testing cannot solve your testing problem in this case.

Case Studies

We surveyed CxO's and senior managers in a wide range of software companies, inquiring about their views and war stories related to manual software testing. Responses and suggestions we received on this subject appear in the following paragraphs. We are sharing with you the benefit of learning from their experience.

Clear test planning, coupled with well-defined acceptance tests at all levels, provide visibility into the management of customer expectations.

Michael Abbott, *CTO and founder of Composite Software*, shared with us the following:

"Software testing in the U.S. has been traditionally not viewed as a priority for many development organizations. Typically, with ever-shrinking deadlines and a demand for increased productivity, many engineering managers cut the time for testing software in favor of fewer features and/or enhancements. This will change during this decade, as a larger focus on quality will be demanded by customers and is already being reflected in many negotiated software license agreements with *Fortune 100* companies. Companies are discovering that the operational cost for poorly-tested software is significantly affecting their bottom line.

"One of the many challenges in software testing is building the test plan with the appropriate test cases to outline the focus on the quality evaluation process. Many companies fail to clearly build a strategy around testing, and thus fail to communicate to the implementation team in the field what has and has not been tested. To address this issue, acceptance criteria needs to not only be a part of a testing plan for the passing of a product from development to testing, but [is] also [essential] to professional services. As a part of the internal release notes, the test case coverage needs to be clearly communicated in order to mitigate product risks with customers in the field. This approach resulted in an increase in successful proof of concepts at the customer sites, as well as more effective management of expectations by internal and external personnel."

Consider speed versus cost in your strategy.

Clive Boulton, *Senior Developer of Exact Software*, shared the following with us:

"Experience is a great teacher. Regarding testing ERP software, including e-Business and accounting… In the past, before global labor resources [were available], we automated to save money on-shore, but found manual testing was more essential and flexible but so costly. We recommend automatic testing on-shore to cut costs, manual testing off-shore where labor costs are not critical. The hybrid of both automated and manual testing are required. Keep in mind, automating testing before a product is version 1.0 is just not practical."

Manual testing, while not scalable, is often unavoidable.

Mark Tezak, *Acrobat Quality Engineering at Adobe Systems, Inc.*, shared with us the following about the problems and benefits of manual software testing:

> "As the areas I test concern document creation for print production, there is not a lot of automation I employ at all, save for some very basic scripting of repetitive tasks. Much of this functionality is built into the programs, as well for the user, in the form of batch processing commands. So the expertise I bring to the task is two-fold, namely workflow production knowledge resulting from seventeen years of experience of the publishing and printing industry, combined with the skills I have learned in software quality engineering. As a result, I am able to not only create real-world user scenarios and workflows, but also to quickly identify a chain of defects easily once a vulnerability has been discovered in a particular area during product development, since I am aware of the functional interdependencies."

Poor funding and lifecycle management leave little room for testing improvement.

Shyamsundar Eranky of *Symbol* shared with us the following:

> "I feel that QA is perhaps the most important part of software development and sadly the most neglected—either due to a time or resource crunch. On manual software testing, even though this is not the most reliable form of testing, sometimes it is the only form of testing available. This was true more so for projects that involved GUI testing than server side testing. Although software automation tools exist for such testing, it is often not suited given the time to complete the QA."

Summary

Manual software testing is slow and costly, does not scale well as the complexity of the software increases, and has lack of repeatability and consistency in results. To improve software testing, you should automate the testing process as much as you can, while allocating sufficient resources for manual testing. Providing the test function with its own budget, as opposed to a flexible portion of the overall project budget, is very useful here. Managing the software test process with as much care as the software development process, from documentation of the test plans and ranking of the tests to test execution and reporting, will also be helpful.

Driving toward the solution

In the last chapter, we discussed:

- The Pitfalls of Manual Software Testing.

In the following two chapters, we will discuss:

- The Pitfalls of Software Test Automation
- The Pitfalls of Outsourcing/Offshoring Software Testing

In Chapter 6, we will present the Global Test Automation strategy, an approach that avoids these pitfalls and enables you to capitalize on the value that software testing can provide.

4 The Pitfalls of Test Automation

In this chapter, we offer an overview of the benefits of test automation, and present the top five pitfalls of test automation, listed below:

1. Uncertainty and lack of control.
2. Poor scalability and maintainability.
3. Low test automation coverage.
4. Poor methods and disappointing quality of tests.
5. Technology vs. people issues.

We will then present the top five suggestions, listed below:

1. Focus on the methodology, not the tool.
2. Choose extensible test tools.
3. Separate test design and test automation.
4. Lower costs.
5. Jumpstart with a pre-trained team.

We will then present some case studies that illustrate the issues.

Introduction

Test automation provides great benefits to the software testing process and improves the quality of the results. It improves reliability while minimizing variability in the results, speeds up the process, increases test coverage, and ultimately can provide greater confidence in the quality of the software being tested. But there are some pitfalls to be aware of. In this chapter we discuss test automation, its pitfalls, and offer some pointers to help avoid the pitfalls.

Automation is not a silver bullet; it also brings some problems. To solve an automation problem, define the test *methodology*; then choose the right enabling *technology* to help you implement the methodology. The chosen methodology should provide the following:

- Visibility
- Reusability and Scalability
- Maintainability

After the test methodology and tools are set, the next step is to put the right *people* in place with the proper skills and training to do the work. The key to automation success is to focus your resources on the *test* production; that is, to improve the quantity and quality of the tests, not to spend too many resources on *automation* production.

Consider Figure 7. This diagram shows the results of a good test automation methodology. Good automation provides optimum productivity to the software testing effort; hence, it leads to higher quality of the software releases. Test automation visibility provides measurability and control over the software development process, which keeps it manageable. With good visibility established, you can make effective management decisions about if, when, and how to do training and auditing to address the quality of tests. Reusability and scalability of test automation improves test productivity. However, productivity should be defined by (1) the quantity of tests (driven by reusability and scalability), and (2) the quality of tests (understanding of what the tests are actually doing helps improve the tests qualitatively). When test automation is reusable and scalable, the issue of quantity is resolved; when test automation is highly maintainable, the cost of ownership is minimized, making the overall testing effort more cost-effective.

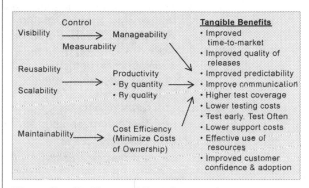

Figure 7: Outflows of Test Automation.

The quality of tests is mostly affected by the training and skills of the test staff. Automating a bad test does not improve its quality; it just makes it run faster. Good test design is a critical, and often overlooked, aspect of test automation. Test automation visibility by itself does not provide high test quality; it merely enables us to see how well the test designers are trained. Addressing the training issues will help in addressing the test case quality issues.

Visibility, reusability, scalability, and maintainability lead to productivity and are the drivers for following benefits:

- Improved time-to-market.
- Improved quality of releases.
- Improved predictability.
- Improved Test/QA communication.
- Higher test coverage.
- Lower testing costs.
- Earlier detection of bugs.
- Lower technical support costs.
- More effective use of testing resources.
- Improved customer confidence and adoption.

The most essential element to achieve these benefits is the *methodology*, not the tools.

In evaluating the return on investment with test automation, you need to look at the big picture. Think of the return-on-investment (ROI) equation, with the benefits on one side, and the costs on the other. For the benefits, consider the productivity, both in quantity and quality of tests. For the cost side of the equation, think about the *reusability, scalability* and *maintainability* of the tests in the context of the phases of a test automation effort:

- Deployment costs
- Test automation creation costs
- Execution costs
- Maintenance costs

Evaluate the ROI by considering if the costs are justified by:

- Faster/more tests?
- Faster/more test cycles?
- Better test coverage in each cycle?
- Higher quality of tests?

To make these evaluations, you need to have *good visibility*.

Often, the costs and benefits of test automation are uncertain due to lack of visibility. Management just does not know how much money it will spend on test automation, and how much it will benefit from it. People are uncertain about how to quantify the ROI and how to monitor it to see if they are on target. This is symptomatic of starting a project that derails six months later.

Excellent visibility leads to effective management of test automation production.

The Top Five Pitfalls of Test Automation

Managers deciding to employ test automation as part of their software test strategy may encounter a number of pitfalls. In this section, we discuss the top five pitfalls encountered by most organizations:

1. **Uncertainty and lack of control.** A very common experience in test automation is that it is hard for managers and other stakeholders to know what is going on: what exactly is being tested, and how is the progress of test development and test execution. This uncertainty makes test automation a risky investment.

   The problem of uncertainty in test automation may seem counterintuitive, since test automation offers benefits that should *reduce* uncertainty in the test results. The uncertainty comes from several sources. With a lack of visibility into the test automation, the *value* of the automation is questionable. As we discussed in previous chapters, visibility is a key reason to do testing in the first place. Excellent *visibility* leads to effective management of test automation production.

   Companies know they need to automate their software testing as much as possible, but they aren't sure how to make it successful. What strategies should they employ? What software tools will they need? How do the tools on the market fit in with the best strategies for the company? Companies want to achieve a high degree of automation, but don't want to incur a high total cost of ownership. They aren't sure how to do this.

   As a result of the uncertainty associated with these issues, the desired cost savings on the testing effort may not materialize. Companies need to unravel their questions, address them systematically, and find answers that will remove the uncertainty and create a successful test automation strategy.

Companies mostly decide to apply some form of test automation to increase the level of *control* over a project, a consideration often even more important than the possibility of lowering test execution costs. Managers hope, by investing in automation, to achieve a shorter lifecycle for the test execution, making it easier to retest bug fixes and apply last-minute system changes. In the maintenance of a system, they hope to be able to re-use the automated tests to shorten regression testing times.

Unfortunately, it is not uncommon for the opposite to happen. Instead of gaining control by having shorter cycles, the automation in and of itself becomes a factor, or even worse, a bottleneck in a project. It is very hard for managers to know what has been tested, and which test cases have been created. To find out what a certain test automation does, a manager must often look within the code of the test, a task that is often far too time-intensive for a busy manager.

2. **Poor scalability and maintainability.** Software test automation can be a costly investment. If not properly done, it solves the manual test execution problem but creates a new test automation production problem.

Maintainability is one of the oldest-known challenges of test automation, and organizations still struggle with it today. Systems being tested tend to change their technology, appearance and behavior. These changes happen frequently even if the original system designers weren't expecting them. Furthermore, the changes often happen in the middle of a development cycle, with very little advanced warning.

To evaluate the cost, the following simplified analysis can be performed:

> **Test Automation Cost = Test Tool Cost**
> **+ Script Creation Labor Cost**
> **+ Script Maintenance Labor Cost**

The costs of performing and evaluating the results are not included here, because those are costs of overall testing and are not directly related to the unique costs of test automation. The costs of the test tool are easy to quantify. The labor costs of creating the scripts and maintaining them will vary a great deal, depending on the test automation framework and methodology. The test tool chosen, as well as the test strategy and methodology, will have an impact on the labor costs.

In addition, having the right balance of people who design tests and people who create automated test scripts has a significant impact on the labor costs. People who are good testers may not have good programming skills, while people who create automated test scripts may be good programmers, but don't necessarily have good test domain expertise and design skills. The labor costs of script maintenance will also depend on how likely the created test scripts will break when the application being tested changes. It may be that additional money spent in creating test scripts with potential application changes in mind will save money in test maintenance.

The following is an example of a common scenario:

- An expensive tool is purchased because it appears simple to use. Then it ends up becoming shelf-ware due to the staff's lack of automation and programming expertise.

- Additional personnel with adequate technical expertise are hired to avoid the tool becoming shelf-ware, but they are an expensive resource. Much of automation production is based on manual test case translation.

- Automation becomes too expensive, so moving offshore to increase production at lower costs is necessary.

- Automated test scripts become un-maintainable and unmanageable.

3. **Low test automation coverage.** When asked how many test cases are actually automated, most organizations will report figures in the range of 20-30%, or less. This has to do with the

amount of work required to automate a test case, and to keep the automation up to date with the latest system changes, as well as the sheer amount of test cases with a script for each test case. Even though some common functions, like "logon" might be common to more than one script, having many test cases means many scripts to create, manage, and maintain.

The low automation coverage is generally perceived by management and other participants as disappointing, particularly when much time and money have been invested and expectations, often based on glamorous sales demonstrations, were much higher.

4. **Poor methods and disappointing quality of tests.** This may be due to a bad automation framework or architecture. The test automation methods may have poor reusability. If they can't be reused, the costs of developing and maintaining the test automation scripts also can't be spread out over the testing, resulting in an overall higher cost. Software development cycles may also be so fast that there isn't time to automate the tests well. Non-reusable scripts exacerbate the problem.

Just as with most manual test cases, automated tests are commonly prepared in advance as a series of subsequently automated test cases. This in itself can lead to uninspired tests, since interacting with a system can give experienced testers spontaneous ideas that then lead to breaking the system. This is usually experienced as a fun thing to do, and is consequently motivating and inspiring.

When using prepared test cases, test design needs extra attention to allow the testers to create aggressive test cases, such as "soap opera" test cases which simulate extreme, but realistic, scenarios. To be able to do this, automation should not get in the way. But in most test automation projects this is exactly what happens—it is so hard to get the automated test to work in the first place that no time is left to make more and better tests.

5. **Technology vs. people issue**. In a survey of all available test automation tools, you may find that there aren't any tools that meet all your needs. You may also find that the best tool for your application is too expensive to purchase and deploy for the benefit that it would provide your organization. In these scenarios, the people you have on the test automation team will need to bridge the gap left by the tools. In this scenario, you need to evaluate the tools with this in mind, and choose the tool that will be best for your overall test automation process, taking the people involved into account. Test tools are generally sold with the claim that they provide "easy" automation, including some form of sophisticated record and playback. However, the implicit assumption is that the testers, even those without an engineering background, automate their own tests. In reality, most testers will not be able to adequately *maintain* the tests as the system changes. Another problem related to the test automation technology and the people could be that your staff isn't using the tool. This may happen due to a lack of training, or due to fear. Your staff may not trust the tool, and be afraid that if it provides bad results, they will get blamed.

The Top Five Suggestions

There are ways that pitfalls associated with test automation can be avoided or resolved. In this section, we discuss five of these.

1. **Focus on the methodology, not the tool.** For most any activity, you get the best results when you use the right methodology. In just about every discipline in business and engineering, best practices are sought out and documented to codify lessons learned and establish bodies of knowledge that archive the best methodologies within the discipline. The discipline of testing is no exception. With a well-designed test automation methodology, many problems can be resolved. This is a key to having successful test automation. This seems like an obvious suggestion, but you may ask, "How can I do this?" We will discuss this in detail in Chapter 6.

   When applying a methodology, it is important that the testers and automation engineers understand and accept the methodology. Also, other stakeholders such as managers, business owners, and auditors should have a clear understanding of the methodology, especially about the benefits that it brings.

2. **Choose extensible test tools.** Select a test tool that supports extensibility, team-based Global Test Automation framework (team members are distributed), and offers a solid management platform. Surveying test tools can be time consuming, but it is important to choose the best tool to meet your overall test needs. Before beginning the survey, however, you should have a good idea of what you need in the first place. This is intimately tied to your overall test methodology.

   Make sure your chosen test tool has an appropriate automation architecture. As stated earlier, buying a tool is not the solution to test automation. Whatever tool is used for the automation, attention should be paid to how the various technical requirements of the test case execution are implemented in a manageable and maintainable way.

Avoid "Record-playback 2.0"—tools that claim to do test automation with no coding. There is nothing against being able to automate without having to code. In fact, it is a good benefit to have. However, in looking at these tools and considering your methodology, you should ask the basic questions of how well these tools address reusability, scalability and team-based automation (a driver for productivity quantitatively), maintainability (a driver for lowering maintenance cost), and visibility (a driver for productivity qualitatively and a vehicle for control, measurability and manageability). As in the early years of record-playback tools, "Record-playback 2.0" appears to be a very nice toy, but its bottlenecks will quickly show as you start getting deep into production.

3. **Separate test design and test automation**. Pay attention to good test design that suits the automation. In the previous chapter, the importance of test design was described. The impact of test design on automation success is often underestimated. Well-defined test cases can contribute to effective automation, while problems with a messy test set will be amplified by the automation.

It is good to keep the automation in mind when designing the tests. For example, make sure there are test cases that verify the flow and dialogs of the UI. These test cases can then be executed early in the test cycle, catching any UI problems which would later frustrate automation of the higher level tests.

On the other hand, the automation should not dominate the test design. To catch bugs, test cases should be aggressive and versatile. Too much focus on automation, with its hardships and required efforts, can easily lead to flat test cases.

Test automation is similar to, but not the same as, regular software development. While in a software system functions work together and are interdependent to form programs, test cases are usually independent from each other, appearing to the automation as ad hoc. It is therefore preferable to use a keywords approach, in which the automation focuses on supplying elementary functionalities that the tester can tie together into tests. This way, the complexity and multitude of the test cases do not lead to an unmanageable amount of test scripts.

The testers should fully focus on the development of test cases. Those test cases in turn are the input for the automation discipline. The automation engineers can give feedback to the testers if certain test cases are hard to automate, suggesting alternative strategies, but mainly the testers should remain in the driver's seat, not worrying too much about the automation.

4. **Lower costs.** Use labor that costs less than your local team, or a tool that costs less, or use training to increase the tool productivity. These are all ways to lower your costs. But be careful that lowering one cost doesn't have a negative impact on another area that nullifies any overall cost savings. In fact, lowering one cost without proper care may actually *increase* the total costs. Less expensive labor that doesn't have the proper skills may actually cost more overall than using labor with the proper skills. It is important to take everything into account, and determine how costs can be lowered overall. In a sense, it is like an optimization problem.

5. **Jumpstart with a pre-trained team.** This may be accomplished by outsourcing; what you gain is a warranty of success and a tremendous improvement in cost-efficiency. A pre-trained team can reduce your overall project timeframe, because you don't need to include training at the beginning of the project schedule. It also reduces the risk, because you don't need to worry about how well the team members will learn the material and how skilled they will be after the

training is complete. You will know these things in advance, so these will no longer be uncertainties. This is an important point, but it must be executed properly or the results could be deadly. Careful selection and qualification of an outsourced vendor is required. Look for two qualifications: (1) a firm that knows more about automation success than you, and (2) one that has competent and well-trained staff to execute. Cheap labor simply does not cut it for this job.

Case Studies

We surveyed CxO's and senior managers in a wide range of software companies, inquiring about their views and war stories related to software test automation. Responses and suggestions we received on this subject appear in the following paragraphs. We are sharing with you the benefit of learning from their experience.

Communicating the value of test automation is both challenging and critical.

William Ufheil, *Manager of Quality Assurance at CDW*, says:

> "One of the challenges a QA team faces is the need to *constantly* sell the 'value added' proposition that automated testing can bring to the IT organization. The value in test automation has proven to go far beyond just testing. As IT teams have begun to realize what the QA team can do, we have used our automated functions as the building blocks for constructing training regions, populating data for developer testing, and even running scripts for the input of larger amounts of data to resolve production issues."

Test automation must be carefully planned. A hasty test automation effort will increase, not decrease, your testing headaches.

An Anonymous Release Manager says:

> "In our organization, poor project planning and cavalier attitudes in development resulted in a huge backlog of testing issues on the back end of the release cycle. When quality issues went undetected into production, the testing group was blamed, and was given the ultimatum to 'automate your testing'. What resulted was a library of hastily-written scripts, the effectiveness of which has yet to be proven. After going through several 'QA Managers', it is finally beginning to sink in that automated testing can't reverse the effects of a defective process."

An Anonymous QA Manager told us:

> "Test automation adds real value. Unfortunately, upper management thought it would be as simple as making a cup of tea; add hot water, stir, and 10 minutes later, voilà—instant solution to all of our quality issues. You have to ask yourself if you are prepared for the investment of time, resources and money that automation requires. There is a large planning exercise that needs to happen. Jumping in at the deep end is not the time to *start* gathering your requirements—that should have happened a long time before you began the execution."

Garry Batt, *Principal Software Engineer of EMC*, says:

> "Automation engineers are always under pressure to produce test scripts and very often fail to architect a test environment. This usually leads to little re-use of code and very little synergy within a team. Sit down with your team and come up with a strategy and plan. Set a vision. Architect an environment that you can deliver quickly, but is extensible over time."

Start with a clear definition of what successful test automation means.

Anonymous, *Director of Quality Services*, told us:

> "Automation has the potential to be great—unless you start with no definition of success. We started to automate for automation's sake and could find no one who wanted to do the work since our budget impacted the tools we selected. We also learned that the type of payback we wanted from automation (functional testing, regression testing, preparation for load testing, product demonstration, etc.) affected how we approached our work. It has not been as successful as we hoped."

Phil Woollven, *QA Consultant of FTSE, The Index Company*, says:

> "Automation provides a value-added service to the test cycle, but should never become a dependency. Combined with strategic manual testing, the quality of the test cycle is greatly enhanced working with automation."

Test automation success starts with good process.

John R Lee, *Director, System Test, Salesforce.com*, told us:

> "Most companies miss the most valuable component of automation: The process."

Pick an appropriate methodology for your unique testing needs.

Mukesh Jain, *Quality Manager of Microsoft*, says:

> "It's hard to test every possible combination. With Model Based Testing, we were able to find the right set of combinations and wrote automation for it—which helped us find the right bugs before our customers bump into it."

Build buy-in from the rest of the organization.

Eric Rupprechtmindex, *Quality Manager of Mindex Technologies*, told us:

> "Test Automation needs to be continually sold to internal groups (management, development, support, etc.) to educate other teams on the benefits and methodologies used to develop and maintain automation. Once all teams are educated on the cost of delivery and the automation team is staffed appropriately, automation will become a valuable tool in your software lifecycle."

A testing tool alone won't solve your testing problems.

Gael Le Bihan, *QA Director of Coradiant*, says:

> "We spent a few months evaluating various test automation tools. Our developers keep finding potentially better automation tools. Our products tend to have more sophisticated capabilities than available test tools support so we end up with a different dead-end after a few weeks of trial. We didn't find any that works perfectly for our needs but settled on a good price/feature compromise."

Ronald Fierens, *Product Testing and Services Manager of DYMO Corporation*, told us:

> "Don't expect that one tool can do it all. In many cases you will need a 'test automation toolbox' with a wide variation of tools."

Automate as much as possible.

Shyamsundar Eranky of *Symbol*, says:

> "Wherever possible, automated test suites have to be created. This not only ensures that your software/product does not regress across releases, but also helps in improving code coverage ensuring better quality."

Smart automation is essential. Use risk analysis to help focus on areas that offer high probability of bug existence.

Jim Nash of *Solidware Technologies* told us:

"Software test automation answers a fundamental problem in many software test strategies: they don't scale. Software test automation brings relief in three areas: execution of the tests and collection of results, selection of the test to be run, and construction of (some) tests.

"At the highest level it's really all about risk management: how to use one's test resources with the greatest effectiveness to approach the lowest possible levels of risk. The secret to this is deriving intelligence from attributes of the software and its behavior. We'd like data to tell us which tests have the highest probability of exposing a defect in the software. Many organizations already have a great deal of data about their software: their problem lies in being able to use this data effectively.

"As an example, consider the development of a medical imaging device produced during the late 1990s. As the product approached the planned ship date for clinical testing, it became clear that there were too many bugs in the software—regression tests were performed every night by a test team; some nights tens of bugs were reported; other nights only a few defects were discovered. Moreover, the design team did not see any pattern to the bugs—it just seemed like some nights were "good," others not so good. After collecting and analyzing the data about the physical location of the discovered bugs, it seemed that bugs liked to congregate in particular areas of the code, while other areas were comparatively bug-free. The team decided that a major indicator of risk, for their system, was the physical "distance" between bugs. If a bug was discovered in one part of the code, it made the existence of another bug more likely. If two bugs were discovered in proximity, the chance that a third lurked nearby became very high. In response to this data, the team went on the offensive. Each morning the newly discovered bugs were analyzed, and the team committed to immediately adding 5-10 new test cases for each bug discovered, focusing on testing code close to the previously discovered bug. Effectively, this strategy managed risk by focusing resources on the areas of code that had been shown, historically, to have the greatest probability of defects. Within a surprisingly short term, the defect rates had both stabilized and declined, and the team had a very rich and detailed profile of how risk was distributed across the software components.

"The automation of this and similar strategies points the way forward for software test tools. We have a tremendous opportunity to use automation to abstract risk "profiles" from collections of low-level data about software components, and then to use that knowledge to guide the synthesis, selection, and execution of tests. We will be able to approach "anti-bug" software, approaching the same level of effectiveness and automation that anti-virus software provides today."

Summary

In this chapter, we gave an overview of the benefits of test automation, the principal one being visibility. Visibility, reusability, scalability, and maintainability lead to productivity, and are the drivers for an optimum ROI in test automation. The most critical element to achieve the benefits of test automation is the methodology, not the tools.

We also discussed that there are a number of pitfalls associated with software test automation. These include uncertainty and lack of control, poor scalability and maintainability, low test automation coverage, poor methods and disappointing quality of tests, and technology vs. people issues. These pitfalls can be avoided or mitigated with knowledgeable and skilled management. Some suggestions for dealing with and preventing these pitfalls were to focus on the methodology, not the tool; choose extensible test tools; separate test design and automation; lower costs; and jumpstart with a pre-trained team. We also presented some case studies from people who have been there and done that. The good news is that there are solutions that can make test automation work for you, and we discuss those in Chapter 6.

Driving toward the solution

In the last two chapters, we discussed:

- The Pitfalls of Manual Software Testing
- The Pitfalls of Software Test Automation

In the following chapter, we will discuss the pitfalls of outsourcing/offshoring software testing.

In Chapter 6, we will present the Global Test Automation strategy, an approach that avoids the pitfalls presented in chapters 3 through 5 and enables you to capitalize on the value that software testing can provide.

5 The Pitfalls of Outsourcing / Offshoring Software Testing

In this chapter, we will present the top five pitfalls of outsourcing/offshoring software testing, listed below:

1. Problematic communications.

2. Insufficient or mismatched skill sets at software test organization.

3. Management issues.

4. Vendor and infrastructure problems.

5. Offshoring risks.

We will then present the top five suggestions, listed below:

1. Build trust or use someone you can trust.

2. Train the test organization, or make sure they are fully competent to begin with.

3. Get a methodology and/or tool to improve communications.

4. Choose carefully what work to send offshore and what to keep at home.

5. Build a team with local leads as part of your team or outsource to a team with local test leads as part of your team to manage the outsourced test effort.

We will then present some case studies that illustrate the issues.

Introduction

Most companies are convinced of the need to outsource and offshore software testing, whether to reduce costs or increase staff. The issues facing businesses are how outsourcing and offshoring can be optimized, how the businesses can learn from their and others' mistakes, and how they can implement the most effective outsourced or offshored effort. In the end, there is no debate *to outsource or not*, it's how to outsource in the best way to accomplish your cost, efficiency and manpower goals and not gain any headaches or stress.

The Top 5 Pitfalls of Outsourcing / Offshoring Software Testing

People making the decision to outsource or offshore their software testing functions may encounter a number of pitfalls. In this section, we discuss the top five pitfalls encountered by most organizations.

1. **Problematic communications.** Communications can be problematic when outsourcing or offshoring software testing. As we discussed previously, an important benefit of software testing for the executive is the visibility it provides into the quality of the product. Software testing provides an information service to the executive. But when there are communication problems, there is a negative impact on these benefits. Suddenly, it is as if you've driven into a dense fog. Your information is no longer timely or reliable.

   Having full communication or micro-communication allows you to not micromanage. The home office doesn't have time for micromanagement, and the offshore staff doesn't appreciate it. The more effective your communication and the greater your visibility is, the less need there will be for interrogation, long meetings, excessive phone calls, prolonged site visits, and other managerial techniques associated with micromanagement. Web-based, fully-accessible metrics, results, and reports are essential for timely and reliable information, along with regularly scheduled project meetings, phone calls as needed, and well-chosen metrics for productivity and product stability.

Building trust with your offshore team and creating infrastructure with good visibility and reporting gives you assurance that the job is getting done right, without the need for endless late-night phone calls by unhappy domestic staff.

What can cause communications problems? One source of communications problems is cultural. For many projects, whether they are software development projects or otherwise, success is only achieved after good communication structures are put in place. For example, many U.S. teams and offshore teams have had difficulty in finding a common vocabulary to deal with each other. In some countries, "no" can be seen as a rude word or associated with failure. Some feel that if "no" is used, it will anger the person on the other end of the communication, so they respond "yes" even though "no" was the correct or more accurate response. It may sound incredible, but this sort of basic communication issue has led to the failure of outsourced offshore engagements. It cannot be overstated how essential ease and speed of communication, trust, and most importantly, honesty are to project success.

One of the necessary ingredients for successful communication is a tool to open and facilitate good communication. In this sense, many U.S.-based companies have had to implement internal business practices that will create visibility into testing. Organizations decrease their chances of success if they wait until an engagement is in process to fill a need for easy and fast communication.

Cross-cultural training for the offshore team is often skipped for a variety of reasons. It may be considered unimportant, too time-consuming, too sensitive, or not sufficiently urgent, or it may be assumed that the offshore team already knows enough. Skipping this training is a big mistake! A variety of cultural issues must be addressed in training, ranging from definitions of customer satisfaction to understanding group dynamics.

Many cultural issues can lead to communications problems. Some of these are described below.

- **Criticism**. The culture of the people in the organization doing the testing may not be conducive to criticism, and therefore you may not get the full benefit of finding out what a third party thinks of your software. Recall that testing is not just about validating that the software performs according to the specification; it is about the quality of the user experience. If the culture of the people doing the testing is too polite, they may not tell you the information you really need to know—that your software is hard to use. And then you won't know until your customers complain to you or don't buy your product in the first place.

- **Language barrier**. If the people doing your software testing do not speak your language well, something may be "lost in translation." They may have difficulty expressing themselves in your language as well as their own, and therefore not convey their true thoughts to you.

- **Lack of creativity**. Software testers, like developers, should be creative. A lack of creativity will impact communications, because there won't be a dialogue between you or your development staff and the testers that would help prevent, diagnose, or fix problems.

- **Lack of versatility and multi-tasking**. Versatility, or flexibility, enables communications between you and the testing organization to be dynamic. Being able to multi-task also is important for communications to be spontaneous and timely. Rather than waiting until a large battery of tests are performed before communicating any of the results or problems to you, a multi-tasking organization will be able to communicate issues and findings while the tests are still in progress.

- **Non-responsiveness**. The organization doing your testing must be responsive to you. Otherwise, communicating with them is like talking to a wall.

- **Non-communication**. If the testing organization is non-communicative, it is going to be difficult to have a fruitful relationship with them.

A well-known source of communication problems is due to the different time zones that the testing organization and your home office may be in. Project managers worn out from daily late-night phone calls are becoming more common. This can adversely impact productivity if you aren't careful.

The expectations that each party may have regarding two-way communications between the organizations may not be well-understood by the other party. There may be poor management of two-way communications between your organization and the software test organization. This may result from a combination of the above problems, or simply because the testing organization is not good at managing their communications with their customers or clients.

Having a local/U.S.-based engineering lead or team, familiar with cultural differences and remedies to reduce the stress and cultural missteps of the offshore team, is very beneficial.

2. **Insufficient or mismatched skill sets at software test organization.** The skill sets of the staff at the software test organization may not be sufficient or well matched to what is needed for

your product. This can lead to poor productivity as well as poor quality of the testing service. The software test organization may not have competency in all the skills needed to successfully provide you the information you want from them about your product. Extensive training in a variety of areas from process to product to "what is a bug?" is essential to project success.

Testing skill-set issues are understandable in most cases. In most offshore test groups, the staff is made up completely of developers. It is well understood that a *bug* as a code issue is often different from a *bug* as a user issue. This is typically quite different from U.S.-based test teams. Your offshore test team needs to have a solid understanding of the differences between *developer* testing and *tester* testing, as well as an understanding of quality, customer satisfaction, and the cost of quality (for example, releasing unplanned patches or customer support calls).

How to test for buffer overflows versus developing effective user scenarios requires different training. Both are essential. Some developers have no interest in the user experience and are much more fascinated by the system-level workings of the code. The bugs normally found at the user interface may be missed, greatly reducing customer satisfaction and increasing the immediacy of patch builds.

The trend overseas to almost exclusively hire computer science graduates creates additional problems. Computer science graduates or developers usually do not make the best testers. If your test team is made up of computer science college graduates, they will not find user-focused issues. Furthermore, if the testers really want to be developers, they won't have the motivation and morale to be great testers. In fact, they may not have good testing skills because they really want to develop code. In some organizations, this issue is a direct result of the designated career path where testers "graduate" from testing into developer jobs. Another common staffing issue is hiring less-than-the-best developers as testers. Testers and developers are usually not cut from the same cloth. An excellent tester may never have set foot in a technology class.

Training is needed in testing, quality assurance, and areas specific to your domain and technology. Some of the skills needed are as follows.

- **Bug-finding skills**. Someone without this skill might be able to see that there is a bug, but couldn't identify and find it. Finding bugs in software is more than a technical skill that can be learned. It is also a unique mindset to testing, with the intent to break the software and find bugs as opposed to testing to prove that it works.

- **Bug-reporting skills**. From your perspective, this is just as important as the bug- finding skills. They need to be reported to you in a well-expressed manner for the software testing to be useful as an information service to help you improve the quality of your software product. Also, how well a bug is reported directly affects how likely it is to get fixed by the development staff. Skillful use of a bug-reporting system enables effective communication with your development staff. Good communication skills in reporting the bug also maximize the probability that the bug will get fixed.

- **Bug analysis and isolation skills**. It is important for the testers to be able to analyze the bugs, whether they can be re-created on demand or not. The testers should be skilled at not only analyzing reproducible bugs, but also in making non-reproducible bugs reproducible. In analyzing the bug, the testers should be able to find the most serious consequences of the problem, the simplest and most general conditions that trigger the problem, alternate paths to the problem, and related problems.

– **Knowledge of the product being tested**. If the testers have no knowledge of the product being tested, they may be able to verify that it meets the written specification, but they can't really comment on the quality of the product. Just as you wouldn't expect useful information in a review of a guitar by someone who doesn't play guitar, you won't get very useful information from testers who don't know anything about the product you are having them test. You also need to think about the turnover of the staff in the testing organization. A tester may build up some knowledge in your product, and that can be a valuable factor for you. But in many countries, employees frequently change companies as demand for their skills increases and companies' needs for experienced staff grow. What may be good for the tester in switching jobs is bad for you if you were benefiting from their specific knowledge of your product, gained while testing it on your dime.

– **Domain knowledge in the category of the product being tested**. This is similar to the problem of the testers not having knowledge in the product being tested, but even more broad. An analogy for this would be having a non-musician review a guitar. This is even worse than having a pianist review a guitar. How can a computer science graduate in India, who has never used a product like yours, develop effective user test scenarios for one? How will you be able to transfer subtle knowledge about your users to people who don't have a remote understanding of the area? How can they understand subtleties about your users when they don't even know the basic issues that your users have? You should expect to rely on your testing organization to know the users, develop and model user scenarios, and look at the application from the user's perspective rather than the developer's perspective. To do this, they need domain knowledge.

- **Technical knowledge**. Software testers should have some technical knowledge and skills to be effective, although not as much as coders. Typical training for testers in India or China is highly technical, which may be great for the development team, but not for testers. Plus, once the testers get enough experience, or the company needs them enough, these technically-trained testers get "promoted" to developer positions and the test team starts from scratch once again. There goes the savings gained from building up expertise in your product that they were testing. In the United States, test teams are usually made up of domain experts such as former technical support or customer service persons who know the customer, and some technical/development people. Overseas, the test teams are almost exclusively made up of technology and computer science graduates. The problem with this scenario overseas is that the testers aren't focused on the notion of customer satisfaction. The benefits of domain testing are lost without the domain experts.

Other issues with skill sets of the testing organization include work habit and corporate culture issues, as well as a lack of systematic approaches to testing. Many companies have found that their offshore employees may hit a roadblock in their test work and stop testing. In most U.S. corporate cultures, we assimilate the notion that when we hit a roadblock, we try again, go around it, try something else, or do something else. This is not a universal work ethic, however. Work culture training as well as trained supervisors and visibility into work production are essential. Systematic approaches for dealing with roadblocks are also useful.

A lack of creativity is also a problem with skill sets for testers. To really evaluate the software being tested, creativity is needed. The tester needs to think about how the product could be better and about how a user might do things that were not considered by the developers. Creativity enables the testers to stretch the product beyond the original intentions of the developers and see what happens.

Quality assurance, or testing, should be taught as a science and discipline in its own right. This isn't happening in overseas technical education programs. Therefore, the testers that graduate from these programs don't have this mindset or derivative skill set and, while being competent computer science graduates, are not competent testers without them. These lacks can doom a test effort. The graduates need appropriate training and familiarity with the user in order to gain this mindset and become skillful testers.

Test teams need to be trained to be effective in their efforts testing your software. Most training overseas is focused almost exclusively on IT applications or using Six Sigma or CMM procedures for internal software validation. Six Sigma and CMM are rarely used in the U.S. for testing. Even most U.S. development teams aren't using these. The type of training that the testing teams need includes model-based testing, equivalent class partitioning, boundary value analysis, and how to write effective test scenarios. A sufficient effort must be expended in training test teams to improve their effectiveness.

3. **Management issues.** Management issues can be problematic with outsourced and offshored software testing.

"Outsourcing software testing is like any other kind of outsourcing: if you use a careful selection process and you are willing to invest in managing the relationship, it will work well. If you toss the problem over the wall and expect the outsourcer to 'do the right thing,' it will fail."
*—**Francoise Tourniaire**, owner of FT Works*

The need for increased management oversight of offshore teams is widely known to be the biggest pain point for domestic staff. Whether it is too many late-night phone calls, not getting the work done on time, or simply a greater need for hands-on project management, you can tackle all these issues with good methods and tools, better processes and communication, and most of all—effective training. Use training to set and discuss expectations, lay out processes and procedures, and most importantly, open doors for greater communication and visibility. Training should support your goal of micro-communication, but not micromanagement. Training should also be used to identify what the team members know and don't know, which sets a roadmap for future training.

The first issue with management is process-related. Just as with any other management issue, you need a workable management process in place. Whether it is in sales, project management, software development, or testing, you need a workable management process first, be dedicated to seeing it through, and then the tools can be used to support the enactment and follow-through on that process. No software or technical solution can cure the lack of a management process.

Many development organizations are very weak in adhering to processes, and get by. But when they begin to outsource, they discover how little process they followed in their work. Once their test and development teams are no longer co-located, this lack of process becomes apparent in the communication and visibility problems experienced by the distributed organizations. Ironically, if a company recognizes this, and actually begins to build and adhere to processes to better manage their offshored work, the company may be better organized and stronger for it. But that's a big *if*, and a big risk. Getting your own house in order is the first step to effective offshoring. Trying to wing it with outsourced or offshored teams without putting the effort into establishing and maintaining good management processes, or implementing ineffective processes, is a recipe for disaster. The project could fail, or miss the schedule, or lose any cost savings that led to the desire to offshore in the first place.

There is a lack of visibility into what is going on with a distributed test team. This is related to the communications problems. It is difficult to monitor and keep tabs on a team far away, just as it is with a distributed group, especially when they are on different continents. You also don't have control over the business processes of this offshored team. Testing should provide the executive with visibility into the software product quality. So it is important to have visibility into the process of testing.

For effective collaborations between the onshore and offshore test teams, you need a platform to support and facilitate their efforts. This platform should enable the onshore and offshore teams to work together productively, communicate clearly, and have visibility into each other's work. Through this platform, they can share and control the integrity of test artifacts, including test requirements, test designs, and test scripts. They can also share test results.

After you have implemented the management processes, then you need to put in place a test management platform and associated methodology. This will be used to track and manage the work done by the remote team. It will also be used to generate progress reports, provide metrics, and control the testing activities, schedules, and risks. As opposed to the team collaboration platform, the test management platform is a tool for management. It provides management the visibility that is needed as well as the control.

Oftentimes, a U.S. company has not considered the management overhead associated with making offshoring work. If you look at the total cost of offshoring, including the extra effort expended by your U.S. staff in managing it, you aren't going to get the savings expected by just looking at the difference in labor costs between doing it in-house and offshoring. In addition to that, think about the drain on your own time. With Asia on the other side of the world, either you or your counterparts in Asia, or both, will have to have teleconferences during what are normally off-work hours. After working a full ten-plus hour day at your office, coming home to say good night to the kids and have dinner, and then having a teleconference with an offshore site can get pretty tiring after a while. Monday morning, start of the work week in China, is Sunday night in the U.S. Do you want to regularly start your work week with a Sunday night conference call? Plus, some countries work on days that we normally do not in the U.S. For example, Sunday is a normal work day in Israel. If you have a few offshore sites doing work for you, pretty soon you are managing a 24/7 work force around the world. With this schedule, how do you keep from getting burned out and stay fresh and energetic? How about your staff? You need to consider these issues when offshoring, and develop some ways to manage them effectively.

Another problem in managing offshoring is making sure your local staff is trained and prepared to work with offshore teams. We have talked about issues with the training of the offshore test team, but it is also important to consider the training of your own staff in working with the offshore test team. They need to be trained in the management processes and platforms that will be used, as well as the test methodologies. If they don't understand the test methodologies being used by the offshore test team, how can they properly manage the testing to ensure you get what you need out of it?

Trust is always an important factor in working relationships. A lack of trust can develop when offshoring test, as well. This can happen for a variety of reasons. Maybe your in-house staff doesn't trust the offshored test team because of any of the problems previously mentioned. If you doubt that you are getting the test results you are paying for, you won't trust them.

With all these management problems, maybe you will decide that the savings just aren't worth the hassle. The overall savings only come when you can properly deal with the issues and problems to make it work. The savings don't equal the labor price differences between an in-house team and an offshore team. All the management processes, tools, overhead, etc. need to be taken into account when computing the actual savings. For all the overhead to be cost-effective and enable you to have savings, there needs to be a sufficient volume of test work. You need to determine what this threshold is, and whether your projects will exceed it.

Another management problem may be that there are no clearly set goals for the testing. As with any project, there need to be clear goals. The goals need to be measurable in a given period of time. To measure the goals, you need to specify what the metrics will be. And then, you need to perform the analyses to evaluate the effectiveness of the project in meeting the goals. Based on the results of the analyses, you need to determine courses of action that are needed to improve. A lack of these things will be problematic, because these are essential for the effective management of the test project. Without these, there is essentially no effective management.

4. **Vendor and infrastructure problems.** Some vendors may have insufficient infrastructure, insufficient knowledge and experience in testing, and may not appreciate your size projects. Perhaps your job isn't big enough to catch the attention or interest of a larger, more established outsource shop. So, you may need to go with a smaller vendor. Does this smaller vendor have the infrastructure necessary to do the job well? Does the smaller vendor have the right level of competency, skills, experience, and processes? Is it a best-of-breed offshore testing organization?

Even with the bigger offshore outsourced organizations, you may still have issues. The offshore organization may be so big that it tries to be all things to all people. Maybe it does not specialize in software testing, but also does development and other outsourced jobs. There are many that do not specialize in software testing. Of these, very few have credible expertise and a strong track record in software testing. Many organizations try to provide a variety of services, but do not excel at any of them. As we discussed previously, development and testing are not the same, and a great developer may not be a good tester. By trying to do both things, an outsourced shop may not do either well.

Many offshore outsourced shops take pride in being CMM-certified. However, this does not imply or guarantee that they have a strong testing capability. The CMM does not cover testing per se. The things that are needed for strong testing capabilities are strong testing skills (as opposed to development skills), domain expertise, the right technical knowledge, and good communication skills. Acquiring these skill sets has little to do with being certified in the CMM methodologies and processes, and more to do with being knowledgeable and smart about testing. There is no equivalent to CMM in the testing arena at this point.

Another vendor and infrastructure issue has to do with poor data bandwidth. Does the offshore testing organization have the data bandwidth to efficiently transfer the necessary data and files between its site and yours in a timely manner? Can the offshore facility receive software downloads from your organization in a time-efficient manner? If there is insufficient bandwidth, you may lose the time savings you are planning on due to the delay in transferring the data to the outsourced shop. In some organizations, the data bandwidth could be so slow that "sneaker-net," or hand-delivering CD's or DVD's with the data on it, could actually provide higher throughput. This is hard to do when you need to get that data to the other side of the world. High enough network data bandwidth to meet your needs is critical.

Also, other problems related to infrastructure issues could cost you precious time. What about service disruptions? Does the organization have appropriate uninterruptible power supply facilities to cover local power outages and prevent data loss? Are their computer facilities properly protected against hackers, viruses, worms, and other attacks? Are there sufficient backup procedures in place? Without proper backups, for example, a catastrophic computer malfunction might take a week to recover from, whereas it could be recovered from within a few hours with proper backups.

If the vendor for outsourced software testing has high turnover, your costs will increase because of the lost time to train a new tester in your specific product and the tests that need to be performed. There is a great benefit to having a stable test team. As your product goes through different revisions and improves in response to quality feedback from the tests, the knowledge of the previous tests performed by the testers gives them insight into how well the "improvements" work. If there is high turnover, maybe the feedback from the first set of testers recommended one change to improve the software. Then you implement it, and a whole new batch of testers test the new software. What if they have different points of view or lack the understanding developed by the original testers due to their experience with your product? Now, maybe the feedback from the new batch of testers is to "improve" the software by basically putting it back to the way it was before. What a waste of time that would be. This is just one scenario where attrition can be an issue. Staff turnover can significantly set back any project and team for a variety of reasons.

5. **Offshoring risks.** Risks are an inherent part of any project, and outsourcing testing certainly has its share. As with managing any project, they need to be identified and mitigated to the greatest extent possible. One issue is that there will be a period of time, e.g., a learning curve, required for the test team to begin to be productive. There are a variety of reasons for this. A new team needs some time to integrate, to get used to their roles and the processes by which their work is managed. Also, the team members need to understand their teammates' strengths and weaknesses so that they can begin to complement each other effectively and efficiently. As the team is formed, some time will also need to be devoted to training. Plus, the test team needs to learn your specific product and the specific test methodologies and processes that will be used with it. This all takes time.

Another significant risk, especially with outsourced projects, is security. How secure is the organization that you are shipping your software to? Will their staff take sufficient care of your software to prevent it from leaking outside the organization? Can hackers break in and steal it? Will someone from their staff leave, go to another company (perhaps as a developer instead of a tester), and take your software with them? Or worse yet, will the organization itself start selling your software on the black market? Protecting your intellectual property is an issue that needs to be addressed. Likewise, protecting confidentiality is an important issue. Maybe the organization won't actually leak your software, but perhaps just the knowledge of what it does is very sensitive. How secret will they keep this information? There have been horror stories of intellectual property theft, which is expected to increase.

The Top Five Suggestions

There are ways that pitfalls associated with outsourcing/offshoring software testing can be avoided or resolved. In this section, we discuss five of these.

1. **Build trust or use someone you can trust.** How can you do this? Maybe you have worked with a test organization in the past and found them trustworthy. You might think twice about switching, even if the other shop might be cheaper. Maybe someone you know has worked with a test shop and they give them high praise. If you trust the one that recommended them, and share their criteria for judgment, perhaps you can trust the shop they recommend. Or, you might want to start with a small pilot project and see how they do on it. If you find you can rely on them with this small pilot project, you can start to build up trust and move forward with your critical work.

   It has been said many times that offshoring forces you to improve your organization and processes. Your offshore team needs to be trained in all aspects of your test process, including communication methods, status reporting, test case management and defect tracking systems, the build process, how much time to spend analyzing bugs to what backup work to do in case of a bad build or downtime, why certain metrics are important, and what they mean, to reduce fear while instilling an understanding of measurement.

2. **Train the test organization, or make sure they are fully competent to begin with.** Of course, if they are already demonstrably fully competent for your application to begin with, that will save a great deal of time. But, you have to think of the overall picture, including how much they cost compared to other shops that you might have to train. If you go with a shop that isn't competent "out of the box," then you need to invest in training. Training builds trust. Take the time required for this into account, as well as the training costs, when you compare options and make your project plan.

   Training your offshore test team and setting realistic expectations can stop or minimize most problems before they cause mid-project headaches, stress or even test project failure. But training an offshore team is different than training your domestic team. Your offshore test team is likely to be more technically skilled than your domestic test team, but that does not eliminate, or even reduce, the need for training.

   You will have cross-cultural rough spots, so train the local team on ways to recognize and deal with them. Tackling these issues can be difficult and sensitive but very worthwhile. Trust takes a long time to build, but is quickly lost.

   The domestic team must be aware of how their behavior will be interpreted by the offshore team. In team meetings, Americans often make jokes, political comments, and open criticisms of management. In some countries this will be viewed as disrespectful and always inappropriate. I have seen offshore test teams lose respect for the domestic team based on conversations we may find trivial. Training can make the domestic team more aware of their own behavior and how it is viewed by the offshore team, preventing friction and misunderstandings that can put the project at risk.

3. **Get a methodology and/or tool to improve communications.** As we discussed, communications are a critical success factor for

the test effort. They impact visibility as well as the overall quality of the output. If they are coupled with a general lack of understanding of U.S.-style testing, they will lead to an offshored effort consisting of only requirements validation and no system testing focused on users that U.S. products demand. The methodology needs to support a variety of test methods and styles, be clear to understand, adequately test your product, and give you useful information.

When evaluating methods and tools for testing (test case design), defect tracking, automation, and communications management, focus on excellent and correct methods, ease of communication, accessibility, and useful measurements.

4. **Choose carefully what work to send offshore and what to keep at home.** Choose wisely which tasks to keep and which to send to focus on what each team does best and to increase the productivity and savings of the outsourced test team. In most cases, your offshore team will have a higher level of programming skill than your domestic team. It makes sense to first send test automation offshore and keep user-focused scenario development and business process testing in your domestic office where you have more knowledge of the domain and the user. Have the home team focus on the users they should know well. Have the offshore team focus on technical-level testing and test automation that computer science graduates would be happier and more knowledgeable testing.

5. **Build a team with local leads as part of your team or outsource to a team with local test leads as part of your team to manage the outsourced test effort.** Have someone who understands the culture and communication nuances of the offshore team lead the project and report progress and status back to the rest of the development organization. Having non-specialized staff deal with the mountain of potential offshoring issues is a difficult task, which will significantly slow down that person's

job duties. Realize up front that there will be some management costs on your end associated with offshoring the test functions. Make it a win-win-win situation, in that it saves time, saves money, and saves hassle for you.

Case Studies

We surveyed CxO's and senior managers in a wide range of software companies and inquired about their views and war stories related to outsourcing software testing. Responses and suggestions we received on this subject appear in the following paragraphs. We are sharing with you the benefit of learning from their experience.

Competent staff is a necessity.

Steven Yang, *CEO of MathScore*, says:

"While at AskJeeves, I worked in the Boston office, but we had QA resources in Emeryville, California. As every developer knows, nearly 100% of talented software professionals avoid QA jobs, which means few QA professionals are very competent. As a result, interacting with QA staff can be very time consuming, and sometimes negatively productive, by dragging down otherwise-productive development resources. In my personal experience, there was one particular QA professional who reported lots of bugs and assigned them to me. Unfortunately, most of the time, the bugs really weren't bugs, and the QA person simply didn't understand the product well enough to know why they weren't bugs. In many months, this QA person never found a bug of significance. I wasn't the only person frustrated by this person. The consensus among developers was that the company would have been better off if this person had never been hired in the first place. If I were to hire QA resources, I'd find a talented developer and pay him a disproportionate amount of money in exchange for the misery of doing QA. One talented developer on QA is probably more valuable than a conventional team of ten QA engineers who aren't very competent."

Close collaboration is needed.

Shyamsundar Eranky of *Symbol* tells us:

"Most of the QA work that I have seen in software projects is contracted out—either outsourced to another company that supplies resources to do in-house testing, or completely moved to another country. The latter case is not always effective because QA engineers need to collaborate closely with the development team."

Carefully assess the testing staff against the requirements for domain expertise and industry experience.

Mark Tezak of **Adobe Systems** says:

"As some of our projects are being outsourced, the tester will need experience in two industries in order to properly test my particular areas. There are admittedly very capable engineers overseas schooled and experienced in computer science, but their domestic industries, in this case printing and publishing, has not yet been able to provide them with a comparable level of sophistication found in the western economies."

Good communication and people management are keys to success.

D. Bechtel, *Intellisync Corporation* tells us:

Overview

"I manage a development organization responsible for several product initiatives at Intellisync. I have teams located in San Jose,

California, and in Eastern Europe. I am part of the senior management team that first brought the notion of outsourcing/offshoring to Intellisync.

"Our own experience began by using a small number of contract offshore QA and development resources. This has evolved into a fully operational and integrated development, QA, and support organization in Eastern Europe with more than 100 employees capable of supporting several key products. We've learned a great deal in the past several years. Clearly a lot of what we have learned is of a technical nature; however, a significant amount of what has been learned (and the area I believe impacts most organizations) relates to cultural, communication, and planning areas of the operation. Intellisync embraces this concept. In today's competitive landscape this is just one more tool that allows us to remain competitive while we continue building award-winning software along the way!

Case

"Communication is vital in any organization. Everyone in the Software industry has experienced situations where a lack of communication with the person just down the hall leads to delays and additional expenses incurred during the product development life cycle. Worse yet, sometimes you are not even aware there is a communication failure until bugs appear during testing. Even the most experienced U.S.-based software professional may miss or lose track of important issues due to miscommunication with other stakeholders or team members. Now, take this scenario and expand it to one or more remote teams, in different time zones, with varying skills and English comprehension. You are looking at a real potential challenge. For example, a situation where the U.S.-based product manager assumes those testing the product have a strong understanding how the product will be used by the end-user lead to several key failures in how the product was being tested by this group. In yet another example, a team assumed the specifications were complete when in fact they were continuing to evolve. Things tend to change rapidly in our industry. Failing to keep key product requirement and design documents up to date resulted in quality issues being discovered very late in the schedule. Desired quality levels were eventually achieved but the delays in the release cost the company real dollars in sales and additional staffing costs.

"There are also cultural issues to contend with. For example, working with a contract organization in Eastern Europe, I experienced several instances of team members at this site simply telling you what you wanted to hear in order to avoid any sort of direct conflict (slipping schedules, disagreement on approach, etc.) with other team members or even the local management this person might work for. This resulted in unnecessary delays. Being the bearer of bad news is not comfortable (and in some cases simply not possible) for someone whose culture has experienced life under communist dictators like Stalin and Ceausescu.

"I understood the significant competitive value this operation could bring Intellisync, a public company, through lower cost of development and increasing our ability for "around the clock coverage" testing of our products. As such, communication and cultural challenges were taken very seriously by our organization. We didn't always "see it coming" but over time our organization developed a sense of what it takes to manage these issues. This isn't simply a new "task item" for your offshore team. This is a real change for U.S.-based folks as well. Learning to ask questions in a non-threatening way helps with true disclosure and building trust. Willingness to adjust your own work schedule to help accommodate a remote team, and setting aside time for daily status calls, IM chats, and other forms of communications helped reduce this churn and miscommunication. It is important to note that part of our action plan was and is to ensure we have adequate U.S. representatives working with any offshore or remote team. Lastly, since changing the culture of any organization is difficult, we felt it was extremely important to establish a long-term presence and commitment to the folks we were working with by establishing a formal entity in the region.

"Our local and remote teams are working well together at this point. We believe there is always room for improvement and our teams support and encourage this. Frequent visits between local and remote groups have further increased the ability for these teams to work together and to "read" each other and solve difficult challenges. Our quality levels continue to increase, our costs are under control, and we continue to expand our capabilities into other areas such as automation using these existing, well-trained teams."

Outsourced testing strategy needs to be thoroughly assessed.

Martin Zwilling, *Director of Technical Services, Fujitsu Software*, says:

"For outsourcing of software testing, if manual testing is proposed as the primary methodology, the effort will likely fail or be ineffective at any price. Manual outsourced testing is inherently inconsistent, non-repeatable, and too slow to be competitive in today's rapidly changing technology. Look for automated test tools, organizational certification in a recognized process (such as SEI or ISO rated), and strong employee credentials in software development and testing technologies."

Summary

Outsourcing/offshoring testing can have a number of pitfalls. These include problematic communications, insufficient or mismatched skill sets in the outsourced software test organization, issues in managing it, vendor and infrastructure problems, and various risks. There are a number of ways to manage these pitfalls. You can build trust or use someone you can trust, train the test organization or make sure they are fully competent to begin with, use a methodology and/or tool to improve communications, choose what tasks to keep and what to send so that each team can focus on what it does best, and get someone else that is local and part of your team to manage the offshored test effort. We will present details of how to combine test automation with outsourcing and offshoring to make them both work better for you in Chapter 6.

Driving toward the solution

In the last three chapters, we discussed:

- The Pitfalls of Manual Software Testing
- The Pitfalls of Software Testing Automation
- The Pitfalls of Outsourcing/Offshoring Software Testing

In Chapter 6, we will present the Global Test Automation strategy, an approach that avoids these pitfalls and enables you to capitalize on the value that software testing can provide.

6 Strategies and Tactics for Global Test Automation

In this chapter, you will learn the following:

- The benefits of Global Test Automation
- The seven-step process of developing a Global Test Automation strategy and roadmap

Introduction

In the previous chapters, we have discussed software testing and a number of pitfalls associated with software testing. In particular, we have discussed manual software testing, test automation, and outsourcing/offshoring of software testing. We have also presented a number of suggestions to improve the results in each of these areas, responding to the pitfalls you may experience. In this chapter, we present a comprehensive methodology to address the pitfalls and create a successful test effort. This methodology entails an array of powerful strategies and tactics for Global Test Automation that creates successful outcomes by intelligently combining manual software testing, test automation, and outsourcing/offshoring of software testing.

What is Global Test Automation (GTA)?

We can all agree that software testing is necessary. We need to test software to be sure that it performs the functions it is designed to perform, under the conditions in which it will be deployed, and in a responsive and user-satisfying manner. We also know that manual software testing, software test automation, and outsourcing/offshoring all inter-relate yet have distinct characteristics with unique issues that need to be addressed. By understanding their pitfalls and suggestions for improvement in these areas, you will gain a fuller understanding of how Global Test Automation can create a holistic solution for your organization's testing needs.

Software testing takes time and costs money. As an executive, you want to have a strategy that will provide the needed results while saving both time and money. The 2 by 2 chart in Figure 8 shows strategies for saving time and saving money. But how can you save both time and money? That is where the Global Test Automation strategy comes in. It saves time by speeding up the test process, saves money, and provides the needed results.

An Exercise for the Reader

The first step in establishing a test strategy and methodology is to assess where your organization is currently in its test strategy. To help you internalize the material in this chapter and apply it to your organization, we have provided this exercise for you to begin to evaluate your organization's current test strategy. Please consider the following questions and answer them for yourself in regards to your organization.

1. How much, in terms of percentage to revenue and/or development dollars respectively, do you budget for software testing?

2. What is your percentage of automated tests versus manual tests?

3. What are the three things that you want to change in your testing strategies to optimize the quality of your released product?

4. What are the three things that you want to change in your testing strategies to optimize the ROI on your test spending?

An Illustration of the Issues

After working on this exercise, you see how important visibility is in making management decisions regarding testing. Visibility gives you the power to make the right choices for the strategic direction of your company. You need visibility into the test process to set the best strategic directions for testing, as well. The right quantitative measurements, test metrics, can give you that visibility. Automation alone won't necessarily provide you with that visibility, but it can help. Automation isn't a silver bullet, but it's a part of the solution.

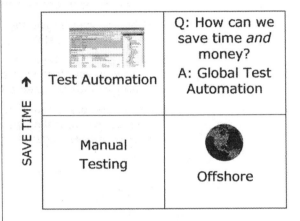

SAVE MONEY →

Figure 8:   The Global Test Automation 2 by 2 matrix.

Global Test Automation is an integration of the latest test automation methodologies and technologies with global resource strategies to fully capitalize on the speed and cost advantages of best practices in automation and global sourcing. That is a mouthful, so let us break it down into the critical aspects and discuss each one independently.

Global Test Automation is the integrated solution for:

- Software test automation
- Outsource/offshore software testing
- Global team management

The main problems with manual testing are that it is too slow, too expensive, and does not scale. Software test automation can address these issues, if strategically and skillfully applied. However, so long as applications are meant for human end users, test automation will never entirely replace the need for human testers. No matter how sophisticated test automation tools become, they will never be as good as human testers at finding bugs in an application. Human testers will instantly notice subtle bugs that are almost never detected by test automation, particularly usability bugs. Automated test tools cannot "follow their instincts" to uncover bugs using exploratory and ad-hoc testing techniques. By freeing manual testers from having to execute repetitive, mundane tests, properly deployed test automation enables them to focus on using their creativity, knowledge, and instincts to discover more important bugs.

Strategy Formulation

The steps in creating an effective test automation strategy are to assess your testing capability, define a good methodology, select the proper tools to implement this methodology, and put people in place with the proper skills and training to successfully implement the defined test methodology using these tools. Common problems in test automation include its potentially high cost and inability to obtain the desired ROI due to a lack of high productivity and anticipated savings. Scalability, reusability, visibility, and maintainability can be problematic.

The Global Test Automation strategy addresses these issues in the four phases of test automation: deployment, production, execution, and maintenance. By providing visibility, the GTA strategy utilizing the Action-Based Testing (ABT) methodology greatly improves manageability, and consequently improves the test coverage and test quality. It also addresses scalability and reusability. These four benefits of GTA (scalability, reusability, visibility, and maintainability) combine to effect high productivity (see Figure 7 in Chapter 4).

The main problems with outsourcing and offshoring software testing include communications problems due to cultural issues and time zone differences and incorrect skill sets. The GTA strategy provides a structured approach that addresses these problems, including a combination of clear, repeatable and manageable processes, appropriate training, powerful tools, and effective management procedures.

The strategy of Global Test Automation is central to its success. The strategy provides a bridge between the problems of outdated manual testing, attempts to address the speed problems with test automation, and attempts to address the cost problems with outsourcing and offshoring of software testing, with the desired end result being an integrated Global Test Automation strategy that achieves both time and cost savings with the desired testing benefits. Global Test Automation makes use of a combination of powerful test automation technology for distributed teams for speed, world-wide resources for cost control, and best practices in management of software testing.

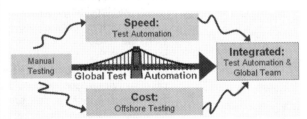

Figure 9: Global Test Automation bridges manual testing with test automation and a global team to lower costs and speed up testing.

There are seven steps to establishing a successful Global Test Automation strategy in your organization. The steps are identified below:

1. Assess your testing needs.
2. Align your test process.
3. Leverage automation.

4. Minimize costs and risks of global resources.

5. Select the right tools.

6. Secure/develop competency.

7. Measure, set goals, and optimize.

We will describe each of these steps in the following sections.

Step 1: Assess your Testing Needs

The first step is to assess your testing needs. To solve any problem, you need to first understand the problem well. The goal of the test assessment is to get a clear picture of your testing needs, what is going on in your current test process, understand your current test problems, identify what is working well in your current test methodology, and define possible paths to improvement and strategy development.

Essentially, this assessment is a data gathering process. To make strategic decisions to develop a winning test methodology, you need the right data. There are a variety of questions you should ask as part of the assessment process, some of which are listed below:

- What do you need to test?
- What type of testing needs to be done?
- What are your test objectives?
- What test results are critical for your project?
- How much time can be allocated for testing from start to finish?
- How frequently do the tests need to be repeated?

While the focus of this assessment effort is on testing, it encompasses much more than your test team. Everyone who is a stakeholder in the quality of testing should be involved, including executive management and the development team. The first thing to identify is: who are the stakeholders? Issues may arise regarding who owns and is responsible for the quality of the product, as well as what the goals of testing are. Different stakeholders may have different understandings or expectations regarding these issues. A discussion between the stakeholders should be directed towards resolving these differences to a common understanding. Some toes may be stepped on, but to move forward, these issues need to be resolved.

We call the strategy development methodology for Global Test Automation "SP3™", which is named after the first initials of each of the critical elements in the strategy development process. Figure 10 graphically illustrates this concept:

Figure 10: The SP3™ Strategy Development Methodology for Global Test Automation.

A strategy to integrate people, practice, and process for success—the graphic describes that test strategy consists of inter-relationships between people, process, and practice. *Process* incorporates the lifecycle of testing. *People* incorporates the combination of skill sets, communication, and morale. *Practice* involves methodologies and tools.

Example Using SP3

The table in Figure 11 shows a number of potential corrective actions that using the SP3 method for analyzing your test methodology may identify, along with what testing areas they may help and what strategy aspect they are associated with.

Possible Corrective Action	Faster	Better	Cheaper	SP3
Automate test execution	Yes	Maybe	Maybe	Practice
Focus manual testing on bug-finding rather than documentation	No	Yes	No	Process
Improve meaningful metrics with well-defined correlation/ corrective action	Yes	Yes	Yes	Practice
Improve visibility into testing/QA activities	Yes	Yes	Yes	Practice
Reduce automated test script maintenance	Yes	Maybe	Yes	Practice
Test earlier	Maybe	Yes	Yes	Process
Upgrade talent through training and/or churning	Maybe	Yes	Maybe	People
Leverage outsourcing including global resources	Maybe	Maybe	Yes	Practice
Improve test design	Maybe	Yes	Maybe	People

Figure 11: Potential corrective actions determined using the SP3 method.

Implementation

A common theme among the findings after using the SP3 process may be that your team is *doing things right*, but they may not be *doing the right things*. This exercise will help you to identify what should be changed so they will be doing the right things. This requires a change in methodology.

The test assessment should produce a report that reveals feedback on the maturity of the QA/Testing group as a whole, and include evaluations of the following items:

- QA/Testing human capital
- Processes
- Test strategy
- Methods and tools
- Project scheduling
- Overall effectiveness

The evaluation process should be based on a review and analysis of the following:

- Current quality-related documentation
- Surveys and interviews
- Knowledge of best practices

The content of the report should include:

- Data collected through surveys and interview sessions
- Discoveries: information that offers feedback on the current state-of-the-practice contrasting with standard processes such as TPI (Test Process Improvement) and TMM (Test Maturity Model) including the following:
    - Process Scorecard: A metrics-based report card for the overall test process assessment
    - Staff Competency Scorecard: A metrics-based report card for the overall human capital assessment

- Roadmap – a plan consisting of recommendations for improvement
- Implementation activities
- Implementation plan

There are three phases in the test assessment. These are numerated below:

1. Intake phase
2. Data collection phase
3. Reporting phase

The *intake* phase is in a sense the initial project planning phase for the assessment. The objectives of this phase are the following:

- Become familiar with the testing organization
- Identify the full scope of the project
- Determine which individuals within the organization should be involved
- Determine what quality criteria should be assessed
- Determine what questions to ask of each person involved
- Determine what documentation to be gathered from the organization for assessment

In the *data collection* phase, surveys developed based on the work in the intake phase are given to personnel involved in the testing and development effort. Face-to-face interviews with personnel involved in the testing and development effort are also carried out. An assessment is made of the testing environments, office environments, and testing processes in place. In addition, a review of existing documentation is performed.

In the *reporting* phase, a report of the findings from the data collection phase is produced, along with a recommended action plan. In this report, actions and measures to be taken are laid out along with transition paths to a new, improved methodology. The project plan along with a timeline and associated costs and benefits are included in this report.

Step 2: Align your Test Process

Now that the report has been produced, the next step in the Global Test Automation strategy is to align your test process with the recommendations generated in the assessment phase. Armed with the data collected in the assessment, take a good look at your development and business process as a whole to help align the testing process. This step is focused on a process-driven test strategy. This strategy treats testing and automation as a complete sub-life cycle with a focus on control through visibility, scalability, maintainability, and reusability. The people part of the strategy is focused on role-based distributed teams, and the practice part of the strategy is focused on methodologies that are based on process and people, and tools that support this methodology.

The activities involved in the process part of the strategy include the following:

- Test requirements specification
- Test design
- Test automation
- Test review
- Test execution, both manual and automated
- Test report generation
- Test maintenance
- Test asset handoff

The people involved in the strategy play a number of roles on a globally-distributed team. These include business analysts, test engineers, automation engineers, technical leads, managers, and sustaining-engineering staff.

The GTA strategy's keyword-driven approach allows test automation to take place in every phase of the application life-cycle.

GTA strategy employs ABT which enables your teams to create a hierarchical test development model that allows test engineers (domain experts who may not be skilled in coding) to focus on developing executable tests based on action keywords, while automation engineers (highly skilled technically but who may not be good at developing effective tests) to focus on developing the low-level scripts that implement the keyword-based actions used by the test experts. This makes for the best utilization of the skill sets of your staff. The tool selected for test automation is chosen to support this methodology. It is a keyword-driven enabling technology.

Consider the graph in Figure 12. The Global Test Automation strategy is part of the product life cycle, from initial development all the way through the operations phase. It starts in development testing, continues through QA testing, and then through post-release QA.

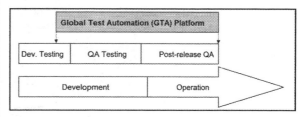

Figure 12: How the Global Test Automation strategy fits into the product life cycle.

The test framework used should enable this keyword-driven approach, which allows test activities to take place in *every* phase of the application life cycle. This approach maximizes the value and productivity of your test effort. Consider the graph in Figure 13. The application life cycle includes planning, design, software development, testing, and deployment. In today's environment, the life cycle is a circle (or a spiral) in a relentless push for more functionality and higher quality to stay competitive. Testing is a critical part of this lifecycle. Without the Global Test Automation strategy, testing is an activity that is relegated to later stages in the process, with no activity in the planning and design stages. This limits its benefits and effectiveness. Consider the graph in Figure 14, where the keyword-driven approach makes this a reality. It integrates testing into every phase of this life cycle. Rather than the development team throwing the application over the wall to the testing team when it comes time for testing, the test and development teams work collaboratively.

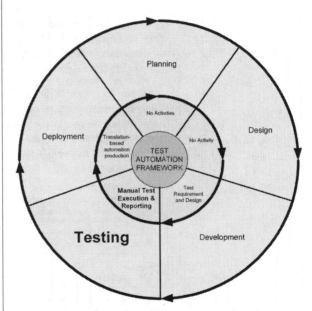

Figure 13: Integration of test and application development life cycles without the Global Test Automation strategy.

Test planning is integrated with the planning phase of the application life cycle. This enables the application to be planned with testing in mind as well as for the testing to be planned at an early stage based on the application plan. Test design and requirements specification are integrated with the application design. This enables test-driven design, as the application design is influenced by the parallel effort in test design. Test development and review takes place in lockstep with the application development. When the testing phase of the application life cycle comes around, test execution and reporting take place. Compared with throwing the application over the wall, this saves a great deal of time. The tests have already been planned and designed by this stage because they were done in sync with the prior stages of the application life cycle. Finally, in the deployment phase, test asset handoff takes place. The work that went into the test effort parallel to the development effort is an asset that is retained, just as the software source code is retained after development is complete. When the life cycle repeats itself, this can all be reused and built upon, just as the application development can reuse and build upon the source code from the prior iteration through the life cycle.

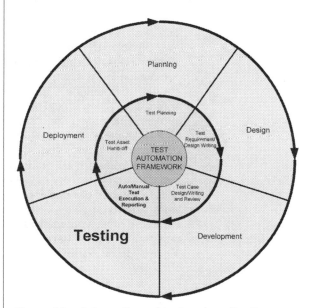

Figure 14: Integration of test and application development life cycles with the Global Test Automation strategy.

Step 3: Leverage Automation

The goal in leveraging automation is to make the most of it and get the maximum benefit out of it. Just as using a well-placed lever can enable a relatively small amount of force to lift a heavy weight, we want to expend as little as possible to get the maximum benefit from test automation. The key success factors in test automation are the following:

1. High degree of automation.
2. High reuse of test assets.
3. Accessible and maintainable test structure.
4. Comparable maintainability to the system under test.
5. Test specification separate from automation.

The test structure needs to be accessible and maintainable to be cost-effective. A little bit of automation is not sufficient to offset the costs of doing automation in the first place. You want a high degree of test automation. To leverage your work in automation, there should be high reuse of the work put into test automation. The tests should also be at least as maintainable as the system under test, or it will not be scalable. Finally, you want the test specification separate from the test automation. That way, experts in test design (who may not be experts in development or test automation) can focus on what they excel at, while experts at automation can focus on that. But at the same time, you want to make sure to avoid any duplicated work between the tester and the automation engineer.

The 5% challenge:
> *No more than 5% of the effort surrounding testing should involve automating the tests*
> *No more than 5% of all tests should be executed manually.*

A general rule for success in test automation is the 5% challenge. The first part of the challenge says that no more than 5% of the effort surrounding testing should involve automating the tests.

In other words, the vast majority of the test effort should be in test design, not in automation. We want to leverage automation to reduce the effort expended in this aspect of testing so that it can be spent in the testing itself. Furthermore, no more than 5% of the tests should be executed manually. So the vast majority of the tests should be automated, yet not much effort should be spent in test automation compared with test execution. This is a significant challenge, and the Global Test Automation strategy has been developed to address and meet this challenge.

To help understand how to leverage test automation, let us compare and contrast the roles and tasks in manual software testing with the roles and tasks in test automation engineering. In manual software testing, the test engineers design, write, and execute the manual test cases. They then report bugs. The tasks involved include the following:

- Test case production
- Test execution
- Analysis
- Bug reporting

First, the test engineer produces test cases by initially designing and composing them, and writing or transcribing the test cases so that they can be executed. In the test execution task, the test engineer sets up the environment, generates the input, and then runs the test cases. In the analysis task, the test engineer performs problem analysis, bug identification, and bug isolation. Ultimately, this process culminates in the task of reporting the bugs.

In test automation, there are three different roles to be played by three different types of people. The first role is that of automated test engineer (ATE). In this role, the ATE creates automated tests, or keywords when a keyword-driven test framework is employed, usually with a tool-specific programming language. The second role is that of Automated Framework Engineer (AFE). In this role, the AFE maintains the framework and supports the ATE's in the application of this framework. The third role is that of automation system support engineer. This is a pretty low-level role which supports the integration of the framework with its test automation agents or third-party test automation agents. This role provides support of custom interfaces, objects, and platforms. The tasks are focused on automating the test execution. There are three distinct approaches:

- Coding-based approach without a test framework
- Coding-based approach with a test framework (hybrid)
- Non-coding-based approach with a keyword-driven framework

In a coding approach, the written tests are coded or programmed to automate the test execution. In the non-coding-based approach, a keyword-driven framework is utilized to avoid the necessity of coding the tests. Instead, keywords are used for test automation, and coding is only utilized to program and maintain the libraries of keywords. In the hybrid approach, the written tests are coded but they also leverage pre-created keywords to boost the automated test productivity and minimize the automated test maintenance.

The ultimate goal of leveraging automation is to create a successful automation program. The objectives are to reduce test cycle time, improve test coverage, and reduce the overall testing costs. Let's say that a new build is created every day, and tests need to be run on it every night. To achieve this, you will need to reduce test cycle time. At the same time, you want to have as much test coverage as possible in the test time allowed, and you want to minimize the overall testing costs while achieving these objectives. The characteristics of a successful test automation program are the following:

- It fully utilizes and leverages the talent and resource pool.
- It maximizes team adoption and collaboration.
- It optimizes all four areas of manual testing, including test case production, execution, analysis, and reporting.
- It optimizes control over the testing and test automation process.
- It minimizes scripting or programming.
- It maximizes reusability.
- It minimizes script maintenance.
- It fully capitalizes testware as an asset.
- It is fully scalable.

When test automation isn't deployed efficiently, by just being used to automate tests that were previously done manually without being part of a new optimized test automation strategy and methodology, for example, it is as if the manual testing side of the wall is playing catch with a ball, while the automation engineering side is playing catch with a Frisbee. There is a lack of communication and collaboration that limits its success.

Figure 15: The all-too-common disconnect between manual testing and test automation.

But when the Global Test Automation strategy is employed and an efficient test automation methodology is instituted, there is true collaboration between test engineering and automation engineering. The walls come down and synergies between the different roles create value for your company. Test automation is leveraged and optimized through collaboration between the stakeholders. This is the benefit of the integrated test and application lifecycles.

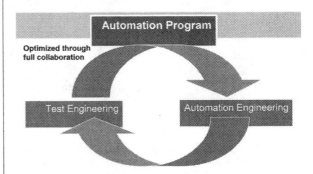

Figure 16: A successful test automation program puts the pieces together.

Case Study: Centrify Corporation

Centrify had both U.S. and offshore teams. They were preparing for a release of a new product, version 1.0, simultaneously on Windows, UNIX, Solaris, and Linux operating systems. Using ABT testing and LogiGear TestArchitect, a custom automation platform was built in just one month. With a global team designing tests within three months, 25 million tests were run in less than six months. Eighty percent of these tests were automated. The full test suite would run in eight hours. They currently support thirty-five operating platforms, and they run automated tests on each platform. Their successful strategy provides them with a short test cycle, high degree of automation, and scalability.

"In less than six months, LogiGear designed and delivered a powerful and global automated software testing solution that proved critical to our successful product launch."
— **Adam Au**, *VP of Engineering, Centrify Corporation*

Step 4: Minimize Costs and Risks of Global Resources

The next step in the Global Test Automation strategy is to minimize your costs and risks. There are a number of ways in which you can do this. The following is a list of some of the ways. They are discussed in greater detail as follows:

- Build trust or use an offshore vendor you trust.
- Train the offshore staff or work with a vendor who provides competent staff.
- Train all local leads who manage offshore resources as well as offshore leads.
- Address all the communication issues, including cultural and time-zone differences as well as technical, English, and project communication skills.
- Use a management tool or enabling framework that helps you facilitate project and task management.
- Have a local person who can facilitate.
- Get someone else to manage and be part of your team.
- Increase the productivity or savings from the offshore team and reduce the headaches of your local team.

In Chapter 5, "The Pitfalls of Outsourcing / Offshoring Software Testing," we have provided some suggestions on building a successful offshore testing operation. In addition, you should use a management tool or enabling framework that helps you facilitate project and task management globally. Such a test management platform and associated methodology would be used to track and manage the work done by the remote team. It would also be used to easily generate progress reports, provide metrics, and control the testing activities, schedules, and risks. The test management platform is a tool for management that provides management the visibility into the testing operation that it needs as well as the control.

You also want to increase the productivity or savings of the offshored test team and reduce the headaches of your local team. A combination of smart methodologies, processes, and tools can help you achieve these goals by addressing productivity issues, unnecessary costs, and headaches.

Step 5: Select the Right Tool

There are several different types of test automation tools available. They are identified below.

1. **Action-Based Testing Approach**—tools that utilize the hierarchical ABT techniques described in this chapter, which focus on embedding the methodology for team-based test automation with great emphasis on maintainability, scalability, reusability and visibility.

2. **Record-Playback 2.0 Approach**—tools that partially apply the keyword or similar approaches which focus on making it easy for non-technical engineers, rather than maintainability, scalability and reusability.

3. **Data-Driven Approach**—tools that make use of captured data to execute the tests.

4. **Scripted Approach**—tools that use scripts to program and execute the tests.

5. **Record-Playback Approach**—tools that use a GUI to record mouse movements and keystrokes, and play them back automatically to run the tests.

In the table shown in Figure 17, we grade these on a scale of 0 to 3 in the categories of Visibility, Reusability, Scalability, Maintainability, and Code-free.

	Visibility	Reusability	Scalability	Maintainability	Code-free
Action-Based Testing Approach	3	3	3	3	2
Record-Play Back 2.0 Approach	2	0	0	0	3
Data-Driven Approach	1	2	2	2	0
Scripted Approach	1	1	1	1	0
Record-Play Back Approach	1	0	0	0	3

Legend
0: Very Poor
1: Marginal
2: Good
3: Very Good

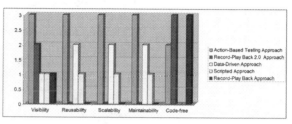

Figure 17: The score-card for the different types of test automation tools.

A well-designed test automation scheme has been proven to reduce testing costs by significantly decreasing the time and expense required to execute tests. The first step in selecting the right tool is having developed a test methodology and strategy that will achieve your goals for a successful Global Test Automation effort. Then, select a tool that will help you implement that methodology. In looking at potential tools, select and specify the requirements for the tool based on your strategy of how your organization will optimally leverage test automation, the talent pool of test engineers and automation engineers, distributed teams such as offshore teams, and the process-driven strategy.

You should ask a wide variety of questions when evaluating potential tools to help you focus on which ones will meet your objectives. Some of these questions are listed below:

- Does the tool support role-based test design, automation, execution, and management?
- Does the tool support traceability throughout the testing and test automation life cycle?

- Does the tool provide a tracking and reporting mechanism for globally distributed testing teams' activities?
- Does the tool support seamless test asset transferring?
- Does the tool provide complete test automation development and QA/testing life cycle management capability?
- Does the tool support a complete integration of testing and test automation while leveraging the talent pool to focus on separate activities such as test design versus automation engineering?
- Does the tool leverage an embedded test and automation methodology?
- Does the tool help maximize test and automation productivity?
- Does the tool help minimize the maintenance effort?
- Does the tool provide an accessible, visible, and maintainable test structure?
- Does the tool support scalable production or a high degree of automation (the 5% rule)?
- Does the tool support a high degree of reusability?
- Does the tool provide comprehensive built-in playback support for many common application platforms such as Web, Window, .NET, UNIX, Linux, etc.?
- How flexible is the tool to be extended for uncommon platforms and/or interfaces such as custom software and embedded software (without a user interface)?

Action-Based Testing is at the heart of the Global Test Automation strategy.

A tool that employs the ABT methodology would address these questions well. This testing methodology is at the heart of the Global Test Automation strategy. Here we describe the model and give a practical example of how it works. ABT will help your organization to do the following:

- Increase your return-on-testing-investment.
- Significantly decrease time-to-market.
- Optimize the reusability of tests and test automation.
- Improve test output and coverage.
- Enhance the motivation of your testing staff.
- Increase managerial control over quality and testing.

About ABT

The ABT methodology improves on traditional test automation techniques by enabling non-automation experts to create automated tests, decreasing the amount of automation scripting required, and significantly reducing the amount of work necessary to update tests after a revision of the application under test.

To understand Action-Based Testing, it helps to look at it in two ways: First, as compared to software development, and second, as compared to traditional test automation. By using an analogy as well as comparison and contrast, it will become clear how ABT can produce superior results while saving you money.

In software development, it is now accepted practice to use object-oriented software development methodologies. The central theme of object-oriented software development methodologies is packaging code and related data structures together into "objects" with associated "methods" that perform functions utilizing the data structures associated with those objects. There are numerous benefits that come from this approach. One benefit is that if there are changes in the data structures, only the code associated with the object needs to change. The object has an interface to all other code which may use it; the interface can remain the same. Furthermore, an object can be used by any number of other objects, creating a hierarchical software structure. Low level functions can be developed once and used an infinite number of times by other higher level functions. Then, if there is a change to a low-level function, all the higher-level functions that utilize it receive the change without any additional re-coding on their parts. This is a huge benefit for the development of large software systems, and is one of the key reasons that software development has continued to accelerate and advance. Before object-oriented programming practices were commonly used, seemingly small changes required in software may have required a great deal of effort because the impact of the changes could be widespread. It was a maintenance headache.

ABT is to testing what object-oriented programming is to software development. Rather than create a single test script for each test to be run, there are test scripts created for low-level actions that are then utilized by higher level test modules. The test engineer will develop tests that utilize actions based on keywords such as "login," and then the automation engineers will develop test scripts that implement "login" with low-level steps such as "click," "find text box A in window B," "enter username," etc. A relatively small number of low-level test scripts are required, compared to the total number of tests that are developed. If a change must be made to a low-level script, say, because a button's behavior changed, only that low-level script needs to be changed. Every test module that utilized it will then receive the change. ABT brings the benefits of object-oriented technology to testing.

Keyword-based test design can actually begin based on documents developed by business analysts or the marketing department, before the final details of the software to be tested are known. As the test automation process proceeds, bottlenecks are removed and the expensive time of highly-trained professionals is used more effectively.

One way that the ABT methodology introduces cost savings over traditional test automation is by decreasing the number of scripts that must be written by automation engineers. In the traditional test automation approach, test engineers document tests, and then automation engineers create scripts that implement those tests. In the ABT method, test engineers create executable "test modules" based on a library of "actions", and automation engineers create a relatively small number of automation scripts to implement the "actions" used in the test modules.

Since the test modules created by the test engineers are executable, the ABT methodology can result in lower costs for each test because they don't need to be converted to executable modules by automation engineers in a second step. And since the executable test modules are written in a clearly readable language, it is not necessary for test engineers to create additional documentation, such as verbose Microsoft Word documents. This can also result in lower costs for each test.

In the ABT methodology, automation engineers create "low-level" actions that handle discrete controls in the application, such as buttons, text fields, drop-down lists, radio buttons, etc. The number of low-level actions needed for testing is directly related to the complexity of the platform the application is using. For example, if the application is a Windows GUI application, it will need more low-level actions than a command line application. In practice, you might expect that a typical GUI-based application will need 30-50 low-level actions.

Once the low-level actions have been created, automation engineers can use these to create "intermediate-level" and "high-level" actions. Intermediate level actions typically deal with a single window or dialogue in an application; high-level actions typically will move across several windows in an application, and represent business functions of the application. In general, there is a direct relationship between the number of windows/dialogues in an application and the number of intermediate-level actions. Similarly, there is a relationship between the number of use cases and/or functional requirements and the number of high-level actions.

When comparing the ABT methodology to a traditional test automation approach, we see a cost savings as the number of test cases (or in the case of ABT, "test scenarios") increases. The cost of test execution for ABT and traditional automation is roughly the same. A test engineer will typically start the test, perform some other tasks, then come back and analyze the results. To demonstrate how ABT can reduce the cost of developing automated tests, let's take a look at the following example.

Example

Suppose we are testing a standard GUI application that uses standard Windows controls and has 80 different screens and dialogs. We assume that an automation engineer will take 1 hour to code each low-level action, and that she can create 2 higher-level actions per hour by building them on top of the low-level actions. We also assume that a test engineer can create 4 ABT test scenarios in an hour. Based on these comparisons, we get the following costs for developing tests for the application:

Using a traditional test automation technique:

Cost of test development = Cost of developing manual tests + Cost of developing test automation scripts

With traditional test automation, each test case will have some associated documentation (i.e. an

Microsoft Word document), and an associated script. The quantities of these are shown in Figure 18:

Test Cases	Manual Test Cases Documented	Automated Scripts Created
10	10	10
30	30	30
50	50	50
100	100	100
300	300	300
500	500	500
1000	1000	1000
2000	2000	2000
5000	5000	5000

Figure 18: Test case breakdown without using the ABT methodology.

Using ABT:

Cost of test development = Cost of developing modules + Cost of developing low-level action scripts + cost of developing intermediate/high-level actions

For the application we are considering, we might expect to see numbers for an ABT approach like those in Figure 19:

Test Cases	Test Scenarios (ABT Approach to creating test cases)	Low-level Scripts (ABT Approach)	High/Inter- mediate- level Actions (ABT Approach)
10	10	25	40
30	30	27	50
50	50	29	60
100	100	30	70
300	300	35	100
500	500	40	150
1000	1000	40	200
2000	2000	40	200
5000	5000	40	200

Figure 19: Test case breakdown for the ABT methodology.

Notice that there is a direct relationship between the number of test cases and the number of ABT test scenarios. This is because each test case is implemented as a test scenario. While there is a direct correlation between the number of test cases and the number of automation scripts in a traditional approach, this is not the case in the ABT approach. The number of low-level actions will reach a maximum once all the different types of UI controls have automated. In this case, we need 25 low-level actions to automate the first 10 test cases. Notice that it only takes 40 low-level actions to automate 500 test cases, and once we've automated those 40 low-level actions, we can continue to create more tests without having to create more automation.

Similarly, our first 10 tests might require 40 high/intermediate-level actions, but automating 1000 test cases will only require 200 high-level actions, and tests beyond that will require no new automation. To see the cost savings of ABT in this particular scenario, let's assume the following:

- A test engineer can create 4 test scenarios per hour (slightly fewer than the number of manual test cases per hour).
- An automation engineer can create 1 low-level action in an hour (i.e. twice as long as it takes to automate a regular test case).
- An automation engineer can create 2 intermediate/high-level actions in an hour (the same rate as automating a test case using the traditional approach).

Using these figures, we can make a comparison between the cost of test development using traditional test automation techniques vs. the cost of using the ABT methodology as shown in Figure 20.

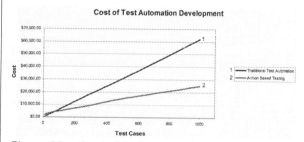

Figure 20: Cost of test automation development for traditional vs. ABT methodologies.

As the chart in Figure 20 illustrates, it is cheaper to test using traditional test automation techniques when there is a small number of test cases, but as the number of test cases grows, ABT becomes far cheaper. In this scenario, ABT is more expensive than traditional test automation until we've created roughly 80 tests, after which time it becomes increasingly less expensive than traditional test automation.

When we look at the cost of developing and executing a suite of one thousand test cases, we see that while traditional test automation offers a significant cost savings over manual testing, ABT significantly extends the cost savings as shown in Figure 21.

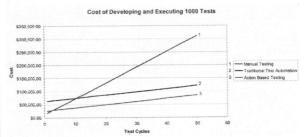

Figure 21: *Cost of developing and executing one thousand tests in different test methodologies.*

Cost of updating test automation after a revision to the application being tested:

Suppose that our application undergoes a revision where 20% of the UI changes and 10% of the test cases must be updated. In a traditional test automation approach, we can expect that documentation must be updated for the 10% of the test cases that are updated.

In traditional test automation approaches, an automation script will typically need to be updated if the underlying UI is updated. For the sake of simplicity, we'll assume that 20% of our automation scripts interact with the changed UIs, and therefore must be updated. Updating a test takes a test engineer half the time it took to create a test. Updating a script takes an automation engineer half the time it took to create it. In the case of the ABT approach, we must update the 10% of our modules that implement the test cases. Since the low-level automation scripts are not application-specific, they will not need to be updated. Since our intermediate and high-level actions are application-specific, and 20% of our application's UI has been updated, we'll assume that 20% of the intermediate and high-level actions must be updated. Updating a module takes a test engineer half the time it took to create it. Updating an action takes an automation engineer half the time it took to create it. In this scenario, the cost of updating the tests is as shown in Figure 22.

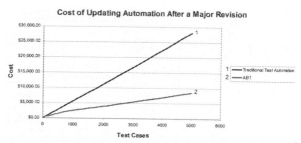

Figure 22: Cost of updating automation after a major revision in traditional and ABT methodologies.

As the diagram illustrates, there is a significant cost savings during a revision of the Application Under Test when Action-Based Testing is used rather than traditional test automation.

Additional cost benefits of Action-Based Testing:

In addition to providing cost savings for test development, execution, and maintenance, using ABT or traditional test automation can result in finding bugs earlier in the software development lifecycle, reducing the cost of fixing the bugs. Since automated tests can be run unattended and execute significantly faster than manual tests, it's possible to get better test coverage on each build of your application.

In addition to finding more bugs, the ABT test design methodology will usually result in more efficient tests, thus reducing the amount of work done by the test developers. The three-step design process of ABT involves defining the test modules that need to be created, defining explicit test objectives for each module, and then implementing the tests using actions. Using the ABT test design methodology, organizations will typically find that they can meet their testing needs using fewer tests.

The diagram in Figure 23 gives an architectural view of the ABT methodology.

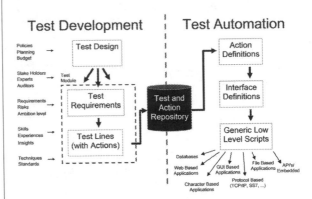

Figure 23: Architecture of the ABT methodology.

The diagram in Figure 23 shows that the test development process begins with the Test Design, moves into the Test Requirements, and finally Test Lines with Actions. This goes into a Test and Action Repository. The test automation process starts with the Action Definitions, moves into Interface Definitions, and then the creation of Generic Low Level Scripts.

The graph in Figure 24 shows an illustration of the scalability of ABT. It shows that for a large number of test cases, there are a relatively small number of ABT actions required, and an even smaller number of low-level actions that need to be generated by the automation engineers. This is central to the benefit of ABT.

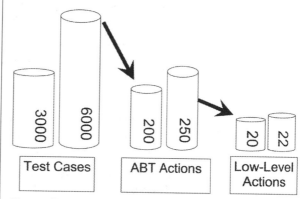

Figure 24: *An illustration of the scalability of ABT.*

Case Study: Openwave Corporation

Openwave Corporation, the leading provider of software products and services for the mobile communications industry, had not achieved the full potential of software test automation and offshore test outsourcing for their messaging product platform. Openwave sought a solution that would provide:

- Broader test coverage and better test quality.
- Faster test design, automation, and execution.
- Better reporting and collaboration among global teams.
- Increased visibility into status to QA management.
- Overall reduction in testing costs, especially test automation.

They chose a tool utilizing Action-Based Testing that provided a rigorous method for development of a test automation framework that could be easily expanded and maintained with each new release of their Windows/UNIX/Solaris cross-platform software. All tests were developed and executed at an offshore vendor in Vietnam, providing improved expertise and cost savings compared to the previous vendor.

Using Action-Based Testing solutions, they reduced their test creation time by *67%* from the previous "traditional" test automation approach, while providing worldwide visibility into the testing effort. Test execution time is now only *seven hours* for the expanded automated test suite, compared to *thirty-six hours* for the previous scripts.

Openwave has *doubled* their testing coverage. Their expanded test suite runs *500%* faster than before. Their overall testing and test automation costs have been reduced by *31%*.

Step 6: Secure/Develop Competency

You obviously want a competent team of people to do your testing, but determining who is competent, and how, is not so obvious. There are two ways you can ensure the software test organization is competent. First, you can evaluate various test organizations for their degree of competency and choose one that is. Or, you can train your test organization and develop their competency. In any case, you should include a comprehensive training program for your test teams to ensure competency and a shared understanding of your test methodology. This also applies to an offshore test vendor. You want to ensure that their staff is fully trained and that they have a comprehensive training program in place.

The following is an example listing of topics to include in a basic training curriculum that all staff members should attend. We emphasize that all staff members should participate in training on all these topics, not just those for whom a particular topic is related to their primary responsibilities.

- Testing Basics (Overview)
  - Why test? What is the goal of testing?
  - What is test coverage?
  - What is quality?
  - What is a bug?
  - Why are there bugs?
  - Types of bugs
  - Types of tests
  - An overview of SDLC
  - An overview of software testing organization
  - How software testing fits on SDLC
  - Milestones
  - Goal of testing in each phase
  - Developer testing, tester testing, and test automation
- Software Testing Skills (Hard Skills)
  - Test execution (running pre-written test cases)
  - Bug identification
  - Bug finding
  - Bug analyzing and reproducing
  - Bug reporting with your chosen commercial tool
  - Test case designing and writing
  - Test case design with your chosen commercial tool
  - Status reporting
  - Other reporting and communication
  - Test documentation
- Outsourcing (Soft Skills)
  - Understand the deliverables
  - Understand the customer expectations
  - The psychological issues of outsourcing
  - Outsourcing models
  - Roles and responsibilities
  - Exceeding customers' expectations

- Delivering customer satisfaction
- Working in a distributed environment

For test leads, another level of training should be included. Test leads have additional responsibilities in project management. The critical aspect that is most relevant for leading the test effort is risk management. An example curriculum for test leads in addition to the above would include the following topics:

- Common Risks (Quality and Productivity of the Work)
  - Test team is not skilled enough to find bugs and come up with good test cases
  - Test team is not skilled enough to analyze anomalies
  - Test team does not write good bug reports
  - Inadequate training and ramp up time for the team members

- Top Ten Risks for the U.S. Test Lead
  1. No or missing requirements and requirement/code creep
  2. Delays of the first testable builds and the software builds get worse over time, cut into testing time
  3. Poor testing and QA strategies
  4. Missed bugs due to poor coverage and/or quality of test cases
  5. Poor communication across functions, up and down the hierarchy
  6. Can't keep up with the work load due to lack of resources
  7. Personality conflicts among team members
  8. Team members get pulled into another project or sidetracked with production issues or hot fixes
  9. Forced to use outsourced resources but not ready to do so
  10. Automation program is ineffective. It is time-consuming but adds little value, and not maintainable and scalable

- Top 10 Risks for the US Test Lead with Offshore Management Responsibility

1. Offshore work is not measurable or quantifiable so lead has confidence it is working
2. Lack of visibility into day to day work
3. Missing a competent lead/point of contact responsible to keep people on task and resolving on daily issues
4. Lack of plans for downtime (power outage, Internet, networks and/or servers go down, virus, build installation problems, blocking bugs, etc.)
5. Remote/offshore team loses access to onshore tools/resources (bug tracking, test cases, build server, test servers, etc.)
6. Offshore team did not tell the U.S. test lead the truth
7. Attrition or team members are distracted or reassigned to other projects
8. Personality, communication, and culture conflict/clash between onshore and offshore teams
9. Offshore team did not listen vs. onshore team did not listen
10. Language barrier (writing/speaking problems) get in the way of the work or productivity

- Top 10 Risks for the Remote/Offshore Test Lead

  1. Information loss in the communication up and down the hierarchy (e.g., did not hear about all changes, issues, problems, delays, just as if test lead were at local U.S. office)

  2. Lack of knowledge (e.g., test lead does not know what the project is about, the users, the technology, how to test it)

  3. Onshore lead does not have visibility into day-to-day work. Therefore, does not have confidence about the work of offshore test team.

  4. Lack of plans for downtime (power outage, Internet, networks and/or servers go down, virus, build installation problems, blocking bugs, etc.)

  5. Remote/offshore team loses access to onshore tools (bug tracking, test cases, builds)

  6. Onshore lead does not listen to offshore lead, respond, and get answers to offshore lead's questions promptly

  7. Attrition or team members are distracted or reassigned to other projects

  8. Personality, communication, and culture conflict/clash between onshore and offshore teams

  9. The offshore team members will not buy into test strategy or follow instructions well, and do what they want

  10. Language barrier (writing/speaking problems) get in the way of the work or productivity

As you can see, there are many topics that the test team members and leads, both onshore and offshore, should be trained in to create an effective test organization. Training and competency acquisition are an important step in the Global Test Automation strategy to overcome many of the pitfalls we have spoken about in previous chapters and create a synergistic effort across the barriers of culture, language, and distance.

Step 7: Measure, Analyze, and Optimize

The goal of selecting and implementing a new strategy and methodology for your software testing needs is ultimately to improve. Continuous improvement is also an important goal in any organization. There are three important ingredients to improvement: measure, analyze, and optimize. We will speak about these three facets of improvement in this section.

First, to improve, you need data. This is where measurement or metrics come in. Measurement provides the data which is then used in the analysis that leads to a plan for optimization. What measurements should you make? What metrics do you need? These depend upon the following:

- What you want to improve
- The relationship between the measurement and improvement indicator
- What affects the measurement

To select your metrics, you also need to think about who the stakeholders in the improvement process are. Anyone who has an input that can impact the success or failure of the project is a stakeholder. Is your software product's customer a stakeholder? If the process does not create a better and more cost-effective product for them to buy, they may not purchase it or recommend it to their peers, and that will have a negative impact on your company's success.

So, you should probably consider them a stakeholder. You want to select measurements and metrics that will help you satisfy the stakeholders in this process. The metrics must also be actionable. You need to be able to make decisions and take actions to improve your metrics in the *analyze* and *optimize* phase of the improvement process.

What metrics do you want to use, and why? Another way of putting this question is, what values do you want to associate with being successful? In evaluating whether these are good metrics, you need to think about why each particular metric is relevant to the "success" value of your test operation. You might want to miss a fewer number of bugs, or execute a larger number of tests. You also need to make these measurable and actionable.

Once metrics are selected, you need to know what the thresholds associated with these metrics are. What value indicates needs improvement, and what value indicates success? You need to use these values as reference points to compare your measured data against. For example, you may have a metric defined as the number of tests you wrote and executed in a given number of test cycles. Let us say your results were that you wrote and executed 2,064 tests in 26 cycles. Then, you need a success threshold. Was that a lot, or too few, and compared to what standard? You may often find that determining where you are today is very helpful as a starting point in both selecting your metrics and setting their success thresholds. This can help you set tangible goals.

Another thing to consider with metrics is the integrity of the data. How much can you rely on the accuracy and integrity of the metric values? Also, what are the values dependent upon? When you get to the analysis stage and optimization stage, these dependencies will be critical to guide you. For example, if you have two metrics that have dependencies on a "knob" you'll turn to optimize the process, but their dependencies are opposite, then your turning that knob may improve one metric while worsening another.

After you have the data, you then need to do a root-cause analysis on your collected metrics to make decisions on what improvements are needed and how they should be made. The dependencies of the metrics on various factors in your process are a critical aspect of this analysis. In the analysis phase, first you need to determine what you want to optimize, and then how you should go about it. There are a variety of things you may consider here.

You may want to optimize your QA/test resource capability. This includes the testing throughput, or how many tests and how much test coverage you get in a given period of time. This also includes the quality of the testing service.

You may also want to optimize the positive impact or effect of the test team's capability on the released software. You may optimize your strategy with this as a goal. This includes both the breadth and the depth of the test coverage. Optimizing breadth enables the test team to test more features in each cycle. Optimizing depth enables those features to be tested with a larger set of inputs.

You may want to optimize production. There are several aspects of production you may consider. First, you may want to optimize production throughput. The elements here include the software requirements, architecture and application design, specifications, and code. Optimizing production quality includes the quality of the deliverables. Elements here include requirements, specification, and code. Optimizing the effect of the production throughput and quality involves optimizing the strategy. Elements here include the quality of the deliverables, the timeliness of the deliverables, and their cost-efficiency.

You may also want to optimize the project management of the test activities. The visibility and predictability are key elements here. As we've discussed before, visibility is a critical element in the management of the test operations. Likewise, predictability is a critical element. A predictable process helps ensure that the execution is close to the plan. If you can optimize the predictability, you can optimize your ability to execute the project as planned. Optimizing visibility helps you to manage the project well so it stays on track as much as possible.

You may want to optimize customer satisfaction. There are many things that this can encompass. In addition to a large number of elements that you can be confident will help improve your customer satisfaction, you should identify specific things that your customers are not currently satisfied with so that you can optimize those as well. Some elements to optimize here include functionality, reliability, usability, performance, compatibility, and security.

Examples

For example, you may want to optimize the project management of your test operations to get your product out to the end user. Some typical measures of software stability and activity are the following:

- How many test cases performed
- Defect counts
- Hours tested against a build
- Code churn
- Requirements stability

As another example, you may want to optimize the test process. Some typical measures are the following:

- Defect aging
- Requirement stability
- Valid defects found vs. test method
- Bugs by severity post-release (how severe will they be once in the customer's hands)

Summary

In this chapter, we described Global Test Automation as a methodology that efficiently integrates the latest test automation methodologies and technologies with global resource strategies to save both time and money in producing outstanding test results, as shown in Figure 8 (repeated here for convenience):

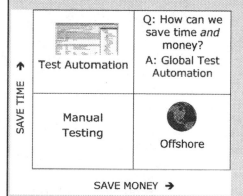

Figure 25: The Global Test Automation 2 by 2 matrix.

You want to view your QA/testing and test automation activities as a complete sub-lifecycle of the product development process, and develop a strategy that optimizes your overall *team* throughputs in terms of quality of service, speed, and cost. Use the seven-step process to develop your strategy:

1. Assess.
2. Align your test process.
3. Leverage automation.
4. Minimize costs and risks of global resources.
5. Select the right tools.
6. Secure/develop competency.
7. Measure, set goals, and optimize.

The core of the Global Test Automation strategy is choosing the right methodology and tools that implement that methodology. We described the Action-Based Testing methodology as the heart of the Global Test Automation strategy. In Action-Based Testing, a keyword-based object-oriented approach to software testing provides a number of benefits:

- High leveraging of software test automation.
- High reuse of software test development.
- Well-defined partitioning of test automation tasks between staff with the appropriate skill sets by separating test specification and automation.
- High maintainability and scalability.

In the Action-Based Testing methodology, test experts (but non-automation experts) create automated tests using easy-to-read keyword-based *executable* test plans. Automation experts create low-level executable test scripts based on the keywords used by the test experts. This hierarchical approach introduces cost savings over traditional test automation in a number of ways, listed below:

- Decreases number of test scripts that must be written by automation engineers.
- Decreases documentation required from test engineers, because test procedures are self-documenting.
- Minimizes maintenance costs by localizing changes to low-level test scripts that are inherited with no additional effort by high-level test procedures using the affected keywords.

Global Test Automation creates an effective collaboration between test engineering and automation engineering to leverage and optimize test automation. It also integrates the test and application lifecycles for synergistic collaboration between all the stakeholders in the overall application development process.

You want to turn you strategy into a roadmap for your Global Test Automation strategy. This roadmap should include training for your staff, as well as continuous improvement through measurements, analysis, and optimization of your test process. Understand that changes, and reaching your destination, will take time. By staying focused on your strategy and its implementation, you will get there.

Chapter 6: Strategies and Tactics for Global Test Automation

7 Conclusion

Introduction

In this book, we described software testing and the top pitfalls of manual software testing, test automation, and outsourcing/offshoring of software testing. We have also described some actions that you can take to improve each of these areas. Driving toward the solution, we presented the Global Test Automation strategy that integrates manual software testing, test automation, and global resource strategies to maximize the benefits of software testing while minimizing the costs. We also elaborated on its benefits.

We would like to leave you with a list of the top ten executive takeaways from this book.

> **The Top 10 Executive Takeaways:**
>
> 1. An executive view of software testing and QA will increase revenue and decrease cost.
> 2. Quality engineering and testing strategy starts from the top.
> 3. You must budget and adequately fund testing and QA as a separate line item.
> 4. You need to create visibility into the process.
> 5. Metrics for visibility are not rocket science, but they need to be established quantitatively and qualitatively.
> 6. Recognize that manual testing is unavoidable, but that you need to encourage automation when and wherever possible while applying the Automation 5% Rule.
> 7. Although automation solves the speed problem, it's not a silver bullet.
> 8. Global software test automation can save money and time and also provide around-the-clock productivity.
> 9. Plan first, execute second—the Global Test Automation strategy should come first. The strategy then integrates automated testing programs and global testing resources.
> 10. Be critical on staffing—don't settle for second-class quality and testing staff, and don't treat them as second class.

In the rest of this chapter, we elaborate on these takeaways.

Takeaway #1 — An executive view of software testing and QA will increase revenue and decrease cost.

The ultimate benefits of effective software testing are increasing your revenue and decreasing your expenses. Both of these benefits directly improve your company's profitability. Some of the key internal values that drive this are the following:

- Confidence in the consistency and dependability in quality through the visibility into the quality level of the product under development throughout the development lifecycle
- More time on development, less time on maintenance
- Effective utilization of resources and budget due to on-time delivery
- More can be done if it can be done cheaper
- More can be done and delivered faster if can be done faster
- No surprises

With an effective test and QA strategy, you can gain confidence in your software products on a number of fronts. You can be confident that your software is of a consistent quality with each release, and that your customers can depend on its level of quality. This is achieved through visibility into the quality level of your company's products under development throughout the development lifecycle. Visibility is a key benefit of an effective test and QA strategy, and it directly enables you to be confident in your products.

When your test and QA strategy are effective, your team can spend more time on development and less time on maintenance. This is because bugs are either avoided or found early in the process so that isolating and fixing them are not onerous tasks. The later in the process that bugs are found, the more work is required to correct them and maintain your customers' loyalty. The more time your development staff spends fixing bugs and addressing short-term workarounds for the customers that are hitting the bugs, the less time they have to spend on developing new features to make you more competitive and profitable.

Effective test and QA strategies also enable an effective utilization of your resources and budget. They enable an on-time delivery of your products, and therefore avoid cost and schedule overruns. When you can complete the new product development project on budget and on time, you can avoid problems associated with needing additional resources beyond the project plan to complete the project.

Effective test and QA strategies enable you to do more to make you more competitive and increase your revenue. They do this by enabling your company to save money on new development projects. These savings can then be invested right back into your company to enable you to do more. Also, the time savings can be utilized for other projects that will also make you more competitive and increase your revenue.

Finally, when your test and QA strategy are effective, you won't have surprises. You won't hear about your customer finding bugs at critical times needing fast fixes and workarounds. You won't be woken up first thing in the morning on your first day of a badly needed vacation with a crisis from the office due to a major customer finding a critical bug. No surprises is a good thing, and can help you to get a better night's sleep.

Takeaway #2 — Quality engineering and testing strategy starts from the top.

Initiatives for improvements in quality engineering and testing strategies have to start from the top. The executive team must have a solid understanding of the quality cost concept. In addition, they must understand their own organization's quality cost model including the data associated with it. The executive team must also understand that testing and QA are not synonymous. The executive that heads up the quality engineering efforts should be fully educated in the intricacies of the organization and testing activities, and must be fully accountable for the quality of the delivered product as well as educating the executive team in these matters.

If the executive team isn't driving the quality initiatives towards improvement, they may actually be hindering it. A highly skilled and knowledgeable development and test team may be prevented from reaching their full quality potential due to misguided management decisions that lack a focus on quality.

Takeaway #3 — You must budget and adequately fund testing and QA as a separate line item.

Testing and quality assurance are interrelated with development, but are actually different disciplines that require a different focus and a level of independence from one another. They should have separate budgets so that the test and QA functions aren't squeezed by cost overruns in development to the point that they cannot adequately perform their function. The way they operate and the short-term and long-term business impacts of their output are also sufficiently different that their ROI is measured differently.

By analogy, consider the roles of sales and marketing. These are often spoken together in a single phrase as if they are part of the same organization and function. But, we know that they are separate functions with separate disciplines and a separate focus. They are generally given separate budgets. Likewise, research is also different than product development, and is generally given a separate budget. To be effective and provide improvements in quality, testing and QA must have its own budget separate from product development.

Takeaway #4 — You need to create visibility into the process.

With the visibility that a well-run test organization provides to management, you won't have surprises. This will give you confidence in the product and service that you deliver to your customers. Software testing and quality engineering are still immature disciplines that have not been studied as extensively as they should be. This makes visibility all the more important for you to maintain confidence. You need to capture the data you need regarding your product's quality and associated development and test activities so that you can understand where you are and set appropriate goals for where you want to go.

Takeaway #5 — Metrics for visibility are not rocket science, but they need to be established quantitatively and qualitatively.

Measurability is the key to visibility. The challenge is to know that what you are measuring is valid and useful, and having confidence in the integrity of the data. By and large, the testing discipline lacks an effective bookkeeping infrastructure. Management of quality engineering and testing should be metrics-driven. The numbers obtained from appropriate, valid, and trustworthy measurements should drive quality improvement initiatives. A valid metrics model is critical to the success of these efforts.

Takeaway #6 — Recognize that manual testing is unavoidable, but that you need to encourage automation when and wherever possible while applying the Automation 5% Rule.

Even when you have a good test automation program in place, you still need to do some manual testing. The usability testing, for example, requires human involvement. However, manual testing is not the solution for short-cycle, high-volume test challenges.

Chapter 7: Conclusion

A powerful test automation strategy is required for these applications. For these applications, manual testing has the following drawbacks:

- It is slow.
- It is not scalable.
- Although it is inexpensive to start up, it is expensive in the long run.

Takeaway #7 — Although automation solves the speed problem, it's not a silver bullet.

Automation solves the speed problems in a short-cycle and high-volume test environment. But automation does present some challenges and problems of its own. The key to success in automation is focusing your resources on test *production* rather than test *automation*. Focus on improving the quality and quantity of your tests, not on automating the tests. Apply the 5% rule:

- No more than 5% of the tests are run manually.
- No more than 5% of the test effort should involve automating the tests.

The most critical thing for a successful test automation program is the test methodology. No matter what tool you use, without a solid methodology in place, it won't be effective. The tools you select should then support the implementation of your test methodology to help you succeed.

The benefits of a successful test automation strategy include the following:

- Improve time-to-market.
- Produce higher quality releases.
- Improve predictability.
- Improve Test/QA communication.
- Double test coverage.
- Halve testing costs.
- Allow for early and frequent testing.
- Reduce support and continued engineering costs.
- Effective use of resources.
- Improve customer confidence and adoption.

The drivers of these benefits are the following:

- Visibility
- Reusability
- Scalability
- Maintainability

An effective test strategy provides visibility into the quality of the software at an early stage, enabling effective management to improve the quality before the product reaches customers' hands. Whereas an effective object-oriented software development methodology provides reusable software modules, an effective test automation methodology provides reusable test modules. This helps drive scalability, which enables automated tests to be scalable as the product and test requirements grow. It also helps drive maintainability. A change in the application that requires a change in the test modules will only require a change in a small number of reusable modules, and all the high-level tests utilizing these modules will receive the change for free. This is infinitely more maintainable than the situation in which each test is fully independent from other tests, and a change has to be made to every test that makes use of a changed element in the product individually.

Takeaway #8 — Global software test automation can save money and time and also provide around-the-clock productivity.

Outsourcing/offshoring provides a cost advantage due to lower labor rates, but these must be weighed taking other factors into account that add to the cost of outsourcing. These extra factors include communication and travel costs, training costs, and higher local management overhead, for example. The around-the-clock test production benefit requires a good working management process to be effective. These benefits require a serious commitment on the part of the local management and significant management oversight.

Takeaway #9 — Plan first, execute second—the Global Test Automation strategy should come first. The strategy then integrates automated testing programs and global testing resources.

The Global Test Automation strategy should come first. The methodology is the key to success. The tools then must be selected to support the methodology, and the global resources chosen to work with the methodology and tools. These three factors must be integrated to be successful. This is the key to the success of the Global Test Automation strategy—integrating methodology, tools, and global resources together synergistically.

Takeaway #10 — Be critical on staffing—don't settle for second-class quality and testing staff, and don't treat them as second class.

People are the key to any organization's success. You want high-quality people on your test team, just like you want high-quality people on your development team and your management team. Don't settle for second-class quality staff. Choosing staff with the appropriate skill sets and aptitudes for testing vs. development is an important aspect of this. Likewise, don't treat your test staff as second class. The test team is critical for the release of quality products. Your company's bottom line depends on that as much as it depends on the most innovative software from the development team. If you want to keep quality people on your test staff, they need to be treated as well as quality people on your development team. You need to get away from situations where test positions are seen as an entry level to development positions down the road, and therefore, in a lower class.

Summary

In practice, there is much more that can be said and much more technical detail that could be explored. We hope that this book has given you a fresh perspective on a strategy for integrating test methodologies, tools, and global resources to greatly improve your software products' quality through effective testing.

About the Authors

Hung Q. Nguyen is Founder and CEO of LogiGear, responsible for the company's strategic direction and executive management. He's been a leading innovator in software testing, global test automation, testing tool solutions and testing education programs for over two decades. Nguyen and LogiGear have helped companies, from Fortune 500 to startups, delivering unique testing solutions which double their test coverage, cut test time in half, improve quality and reduce cost. As one of the top thought-leaders in the software testing industry, Nguyen is coauthor of the top-selling book in the software testing field, Testing Computer Software (Wiley, 2nd ed. 2002) and other publications including Testing Applications on the Web (Wiley, 2nd ed. 2003). Nguyen's experience includes leadership roles in software development, quality, and product management at leading software companies.

Nguyen is also a director of two non-profit organizations, the Association for Software Testing, an organization dedicated to improving the practice of software testing by advancing the science of testing and its application which he co-founded, and San Francisco Bay Jazz Ensemble, an eighteen-piece big band with a mission to provide live music to local community as well as through international venues to further public awareness and appreciation of the valuable American musical heritage, jazz. He holds a Bachelor of Science in Quality Assurance from Cogswell Polytechnical College.

Michael Hackett co-founded LogiGear in 1994 and leads the company's LogiGear University training operations division, setting the standard in software testing education programs for many of the world's leading software development organizations. Mr. Hackett is coauthor of the popular Testing Applications on the Web (Wiley, 2nd ed. 2003), and has helped many clients produce, test and deploy applications ranging from business productivity to educational multimedia across multiple platforms and multiple language editions. His clients have included Palm Computing, Oracle, CNET, Roche Pharmaceuticals, Pfizer and Bank of America.

He is on the Board of Advisors for the Software Quality Engineering and Management Certificate Program at University of California at Santa Cruz. Michael's training has brought Silicon Valley Quality and Testing Expertise to 10 countries around the world. He holds a Bachelor of Science in Engineering from Carnegie-Mellon University.

Brent K. Whitlock is a Program Manager at Digidesign, a division of Avid Technology, Inc. He continues to consult as needed with RSoft Design Group, which he joined as a partner in 1998 and acted in the roles of Director of Optical Systems Research and Business Development. He initiated and led the development and commercialization of several optical communication system simulation software packages including LinkSIM™, ModeSYS™, and OptSim™ 4, which won the Lightwave OFC/NFOEC 2005 Attendees' Choice Award. He has also secured and served as Principal Investigator on federally funded SBIR, STTR, and NIST ATP research contracts.

Dr. Whitlock earned his BS, MS, and PhD degrees all in Electrical Engineering from the University of Illinois at Urbana-Champaign. Dr. Whitlock has co-authored over 30 technical papers and articles, served on a program committee and as session chair for several technical conferences, and been active in industry standards bodies including the TIA, IEEE, and SAE. He is a Senior Member of the IEEE and Chair of the Santa Clara Valley chapter of IEEE LEOS.

About LogiGear®

LogiGear is the leading provider of global solutions for software testing, focusing on test automation. Founded in 1994, led by top thought leaders in the software testing industry, and supported by a bright, hard-working staff that has a passion for software testing, and that all-important eye for detail, LogiGear has provided effective software quality solutions to clients ranging from the Fortune 500 to early-stage startups. LogiGear works closely with its customers to determine their exact software quality testing goals and challenges, then designs unique solutions based on our onshore/offshore testing services, test automation tools, QA training, and consulting.

LogiGear partners with its customers to ensure that they have the right approach for test automation success. Based on the unique goals and needs of an organization, LogiGear provides varying solutions such as a complete Global Test Automation solution, Action Based Testing™ training, consulting, coaching, TestArchitect tooling or integration of existing third-party or homegrown tools into the TestArchitect framework.

LogiGear is a privately funded corporation headquartered in Foster City, California.

About TestArchitect™

TestArchitect provides a powerful test automation framework supporting the Action Based Testing™ method, allowing software development teams to double their test coverage and decrease testing time, leading to better product quality and reduced costs.

TestArchitect is flexible and easy-to-use, and draws on LogiGear's many years of experience in the software quality assurance industry, including the leadership of the original architect of the keyword driven testing method. LogiGear offers turnkey test automation solutions that will benefit the entire software quality process, from test design to team management.

Reducing time-to-market and improving product quality are critical to the success of any software organization. TestArchitect enables all members of the team to improve the testing effort. Testers and business analysts have an easy-to-use method for creating intelligent, maintainable tests which can be executed manually or automatically. Automation engineers have powerful tools based on industry-standard languages for creating the underlying test automation. Managers can maintain control and efficiency of their global testing efforts through a central repository and easy-to-use, customizable reports. Business stakeholders can reduce testing cost through our proven ROI model.